8.

Einei Hashem

Einei Hashem

Contemporary Stories of Divine Providence
in Eretz Yisrael

by DR. MEIR WIKLER

FELDHEIM PUBLISHERS
JERUSALEM · NEW YORK

First published 1997

Copyright © 1997 by Meir Wikler

ISBN 0-87306-852-1

FELDHEIM PUBLISHERS
POB 35002 / Jerusalem, Israel

200 Airport Executive Park
Nanuet, NY 10954

10 9 8 7 6 5 4 3

Printed in Israel

This book is dedicated
in loving memory to my father-in-law,

Hachaver, R' Shlomo ben Yisroel Meir Ferber ז״ל

a paragon of humility
whose life was devoted to
performing _chesed_ and pursuing peace,
who loved me more than a son,
who never let the tiniest favor
go unappreciated, who always
relished listening to my stories
as much as I enjoyed telling them,
and who taught me by example
how to live with a deep awareness
and appreciation of _hashgachah pratis_
in daily life.

_"...And what does Hashem want from you:
only doing justice, loving kindness,
and walking humbly with your God."_

MICHAH 6:8

Rabbi CHAIM P. SCHEINBERG

Rosh Hayeshiva "TORAH-ORE"

and Morah Hora'ah of Kiryat Mattersdorf

הרב חיים פינחס שיינברג

ראש ישיבת "תורה-אור"

ומורה הוראה דקרית מטרסדורף

בס"ד

Rosh Chodesh Nisan, 5757

Emunah in *hashgachah pratis* is one of the most fundamental tenets of *Yiddishkeit*. The Rambam, for example, lists it first among his thirteen principles of faith. And as the *Sefer Ha-Chinnuch* writes, "A person should know and pay attention to the fact that everything that happens to him, whether for good or bad, comes to him from Hashem,... There can be nothing without the Will of Hashem" (*Parashas Kedoshim*, mitzvah 241).

Einei Hashem: Contemporary Stories of Divine Providence in Eretz Yisrael is designed to strengthen our *emunah* in *hashgachah pratis*. All who read these inspirational stories will deepen and enrich their awareness of *hashgachah pratis* in daily life.

This is Dr. Meir Wikler's third *sefer*. What I have written in his first two publications is even more evident in the pages of this latest volume: "The author is a true *ben Torah* and it is clear from this *sefer* that his *yiras Shamayim* has not been compromised by his professionalism."

As Shlomo *Ha-Melech* declared, "*Chut ha-meshulash lo bim'heira yinatek* — A three-ply rope will not unravel quickly" (*Koheles* 4:12). May Dr. Wikler see much *hatzlachah* from all three of his *sefarim*.

Rabbi Chaim P. Scheinberg

רחוב פנים מאירות 2, ירושלים, ת. ד. 6979, טל. 371513-(02), ישראל

2, Panim Meirot St., Jerusalem, P. O. B. 6 9 7 9, Tel (02)-371513, Israel

הרב לוי יצחק הלוי הורוויץ

בן הרה"צ פינחס דוד זצוק"ל · דער באסטאנער רבי

Grand Rabbi Levi Y. Horowitz

מוסדות בוסטון בארה"ק
בנשיאות האדמו"ר שליט"א
מעלות האדמו"ר מבוסטון ז
הר נוף, ירושלים Israel

כ"ט ניסן תשנ"ז

In demonstrating his talent to visualize ideas through the recitation of stories, my friend Dr. Meir Wikler has again done so with the concept of השגחה פרטית (Divine intervention)

The great Chasidic Rebbes have always used stories to emphasize their concepts. The שבחי הבעש"ט tells us that the Baal Shem Tov and his disciples were unsure of the way to a certain town. They then met a non-Jewish traveler whom they asked for directions. Instead of guiding them his reply was, "Gentlemen, you are lost." The Holy Baal Shem Tov told his disciples that this was in fact a message from Heaven that they were lost in their spiritual path of this world.

The Medrash tells us that Avraham Avinu discovered G-D when he asked: Can it be that the "בירה" - "the world" has no Master? Then Hashem revealed himself to Avraham and told him that he in fact was the בעל הבירה. This statement emphasizes that in order to see Hashgacha Pratis one must actively search to find the Master of the world in every occurrence.

Reb Meir has done so in presenting some beautiful stories and reaching out to emphasize the aspect of Divine Intervention in all that is life, thus giving us the opportunity of looking for the בעל הבירה and locating Him.

May we be זוכה to find our path and discover our Master.

The Bostoner Rebbe

שלמה ברעוודה

בעמח״ס להודות ולהלל,
קימו וקבלו, ליל שמורים,
איפה שלמה על פירושי הגר״א.

7 Nisan, 5757

The Jewish people have suffered countless physical hardships for centuries. However, the spiritual damage done to our people in the *Galus* is far more significant. The practice of numerous mitzvos has weakened considerably, as is well known. Alas, even the knowledge of some of the basic foundations of our faith is lacking amongst many of our brethren.

The Talmud teaches us (*Makkos* 24a) that the foundation of all 613 mitzvos in embodied in the words of the prophet Habakuk: "and a *tzaddik* (righteous person) shall live by his *emunah* (true faith in the Almighty)" (2:4).

Therefore, the Rambam writes that of all his numerous Torah writings, he feels the greatest satisfaction when explaining a principle of *emunah*.

Dr. Meir Wikler's courageous devotion to the true values of Torah is unique in our times. He does battle with letters to the editors of famous newspapers and periodicals when they attack Orthodox Jewry. He has published numerous essays and articles of his own on topics truly vital for preserving and enhancing the practice of Torah and mitzvos amongst our people. He has authored major works, including a book on *shalom bayis* (marital harmony and related topics) and another book dealing with true Jewish hospitality.

Presently, Dr. Wikler has produced a book of extreme importance, *Einei Hashem*, to strengthen true *emunah*, the pillar upon which Torah and mitzvos rest securely. The book contains a collection of true stories, beautifully written, about daily occurrences in Eretz Yisroel, in which the hand of the Almighty is clearly visible.

Dr. Wikler and his family should be blessed and strengthened by Hashem, for the added strength that his writings have given to the Jewish people, in *emunah* and in Torah practice.

Sincerely,
Shlomo Brevda

AARON D. TWERSKI

PROFESSOR OF LAW

AREA CODE 718

780-7999

FAX No.

718-802-1581

7 Adar, 5757

My good friend and *chavrusa*, Dr. Meir Wikler, has once again taken pen in hand to warm the hearts of *Klal Yisroel* and strengthen their deep trust and faith in Hashem. The hallmark of a good psychologist is the ability to listen. What separates the truly excellent therapist from the ordinary is that the master can hear strains in the soul that others simply don't pick up.

Dr. Wikler possesses not only an *ayin yafah* but also an *ozen yafah*. He listens to stories that might easily pass the attention of most but he hears and sees in them different strains. So we now have before us a book dealing with contemporary stories of *hashgachah pratis* (Divine Providence). For the most part they happened to ordinary, often simple, Jews. But, each gives testimony that the *Ribbono shel Olam* (the Master of the Universe) oversees and ordains our every step. We have been privileged to benefit from Dr. Wikler's very sensitive ear and from his own deep and abiding faith in Hashem.

May Hashem grant that in the *zechus* of the *emunah* that he instills in the hearts of *Bnei Yisroel*, that he and his family be granted *simchah* and *nachas* so that he may, with a heart full of joy, be able to hear the melody of true *bitachon* and relate it to us time and again in the years to come.

Aaron D. Twerski

THE JEWISH OBSERVER

A Journal of Jewish Thought

June 2, 1997

26 Iyar, 5757

One of the most elusive commands in the Torah is that which bids us to "Place...[G-d's] words upon your heart," instructing us to *feel* that which we believe. One wonders: How can emotions be legislated?

But with the demand comes an approach. And one of the most effective routes from the mind to the heart is a good story. It is thus with a sense of excitement and gratification that one picks up Meir Wikler's book, *Einei Hashem*, to read — no, to *experience* — how one actually feels the Hand of Hashem, as it were, in the otherwise ordinary flow of events — ordinary except for the fact that their setting is in Eretz Yisroel, where "the Eyes of the L-rd are focused" throughout the year.

These stories, one and all true incidents in the lives of real people, are experiences that pave the road from the mind to the heart with joy and fulfillment, strengthening the reader's *emunah* every inch of the way.

It is so rewarding to find good writing, great story telling and inspiring instruction, all interwoven on every page of the same book.

Rabbi Nisson Wolpin

Editor

About the Author

Dr. Meir Wikler is a psychotherapist and family counselor in full-time private practice in Brooklyn, New York. He has published over three dozen articles in lay and professional periodicals, and is also the author of *The First Seven Days: A Practical Guide to the Traditional Observance of Shiva for Mourners, Their Families and Friends* (United Hebrew Community, 1987); *Bayis Ne'eman b'Yisrael: Practical Steps to Success in Marriage* (Feldheim Publishers, 1988); and *AiSHeL: Stories of Contemporary Jewish Hospitality* (Feldheim, 1994).

Dr. Wikler has lectured extensively to both lay and professional audiences on mental health and family life in the Orthodox community. His clinical work has been featured in several newspapers, including *The New York Times* and *The Jerusalem Post*, and he is listed in *Who's Who in World Jewry*.

Contents

Acknowledgments

Even I Never Envisioned I would write a book about *hash-gachah pratis*. It is a *zechus* for which I am deeply grateful to *Hashem Yisborach*. In addition, I appreciate having had the *zechus* of visiting Eretz Yisrael many times.

I am also thankful for the *hashgachah pratis* of having met, found or bumped into all those people who told me the remarkable stories included here: David Amuyal, Shmuel and Tova Ben David, Rabbi Nochum Cohen, Rabbi Yom Tov Cohen, Rabbi Matisyahu Danziger, Rabbi Mordechai Dolinsky, Zelig Dolinsky, Rabbi Leizer Feinberg, Yaakov Feldheim, Rabbi Dovid Finkelman, Rabbi Dovid Gottlieb, Mayer Isaacs, Aryeh Jacobi, Rabbi Zev Jacobs, Rabbi Zvi Kesser, Rabbi Zev Leff, Rabbi Yona Levy, Rabbi Yerachmiel Milstein, Rabbi Zelig Pliskin, Rabbi Akiva Solomon, Rabbi Nossi Spitzer, Rabbi Hanoch Teller, and Rabbi Benjamin Yudin.

Other people have also contributed to this book and without them its publication would not have been possible. I welcome this opportunity to express my gratitude to:

GRAND RABBI LEVI I. HOROWITZ, the Bostoner Rebbe, *shlita*, for his lifelong inspiration, guiding hand, boundless *chesed*, and intimate concern for me and all members of my family; and for his laudatory letter of *haskamah*;

HAGAON HARAV CHAIM P. SCHEINBERG, *shlita*, Rosh Ha-Yeshivah, Torah Ore and *Mora d'Asra*, Kiryat Mattersdorf, for his prennially open door and for his gracious letter of *haskamah*;

HARAV NOACH WEINBERG, *shlita*, Rosh Ha-Yeshivah, Yeshivah Aish Hatorah, for the inspiration that led to my writing this book (see Preface) and for sharing with me three extraordinary stories (see "Meeting with a Master").

HARAV SHLOMO BREVDA, *shlita*, for his inspiring *shiurim*, wise counsel, and tender guidance in both *inyanei d'alma* and *inyanei d'Shemaya*, and for his generous and kind letter of *haskamah*;

RABBI NISSON WOLPIN, editor of *The Jewish Observer*, for his expert editorial coaching on many of my publications and for his warm letter of *haskamah*;

RABBI DR. AARON D. TWERSKI, Professor of Law at Brooklyn Law School and fromer Dean of Hofstra Law School, for his cherished friendship and treasured *chavrusoschaft*, and for his profound and eloquent letter of *haskamah*;

RABBI PAYSACH KROHN, *mohel*, author, world-wide lecturer, and valued friend, for his unique insights and constructive criticism of this manuscript and for his enthusiastic support and encouragement along the way;

RABBI YOSEF WIKLER, *Menahel,* Yeshivah Birkas Reuven, and editor and publisher of *Kashrus Magazine*, for his thoughtful and benevolent fraternal guidance on this and other projects and for teaching me much more than simply, *"v'es l'rabbos achicha ha-gadol"*;

RABBI YAAKOV SALOMON, C.S.W., psychotherapist, author, lecturer, director of Discovery Seminars, dear friend and *yedid ne'eman*, for his priceless and creative contributions to this book, as well as all aspects of my professional career, and for his uncompromising personal commitment to me both in times of joy and times of challenge;

YAAKOV and YITZCHOK FELDHEIM, of Feldheim Publishers, for their editorial and marketing talents, their initial vote of confidence in making me a published author, and for their patient tolerance of my compulsivity and perfectionism;

The editorial, design, and production staff of Feldheim Publishers, especially: MRS. MARSI TABAK, editorial director; JOYCE BENNETT, for her careful editing of this manuscript; HARVEY KLINEMAN, art director, for his design of the book and the cover; and HANNAH HARTMAN, for her typesetting and for her helpful suggestions.

SARAH WIKLER, my daughter, for surrendering many turns

at the computer so that I could write these stories, for giving up her time with her father so that I could complete this manuscript, and for encouraging me with her pride in my work;

YESHAYA WIKLER, my son, for covering up his boredom whenever his father met a potential source for another *hashgachah pratis* story, for giving up his time with his father so that I could complete this manuscript, and for encouraging me with his pride in my work;

"*Acharon, acharon, chaviv*" (the best is saved for last), my dear wife, MALKA, for her painstaking review of each draft of the manuscript, and for her faithful support and patient indulgence throughout my career for which she deserves all of the credit for whatever I have accomplished, *b'ezras Hashem*. Of her it may be said, "That which is mine and that which is yours all belong to her" (*Kesubbos* 63a).

Preface

It was a notice that I saw on a lamppost in Yerushalayim, about fifteen years ago, that eventually led me to write this book.

The flyer announced that Rabbi Noach Weinberg, *shlita,* the *Rosh Yeshivah* of Aish Hatorah, would be delivering a public lecture in English on "*Kiruv* Skills for the Non-Professional." Intrigued by the title, I decided to attend.

In his charismatic style, Rabbi Weinberg kept the audience of approximately 400 men spellbound for over two hours. Weaving one story into another, Rabbi Weinberg presented a colorful tapestry of Torah insights, personal anecdotes, and practical interpersonal techniques. The message was clear: Everyone is capable of influencing each non-observant Jew he meets — and he should always try to do so.

One concrete suggestion which has remained with me since then was, "Keep a personal diary of miracles." As Rabbi Weinberg explained, even non-committed Jews believe in miracles. They believe that some events are so amazing that they cannot be explained by chance or coincidence. They can accept that Heaven has intervened. What they may find difficult to accept, however, is that all such stories are really true. Therefore, concluded Rabbi Weinberg, if you keep a journal of miracles that happened to *you*, then your non-religious friend will be more inclined to accept the veracity of the miracles.

Rabbi Weinberg, of course, did not invent the idea of keeping a personal journal of miraculous events. It is well known, for example, that the late *Mashgiach* of the Mirrer Yeshivah, Rabbi Chazkel Levenstein, *zatzal*, frequently encouraged his *talmidim* to keep their own diaries of personally

1

witnessed miracles. In this way, he taught, others would be able to strengthen their own belief in Divine Providence.

Following Rabbi Weinberg's suggestion, I have kept my own journal of personal miracles, many of which took place during visits to Eretz Yisrael.

More recently, I began to ask my friends for accounts of their own personal miracles, and I soon discovered that many of their stories also took place in Eretz Yisrael.

While pondering this "coincidence," I recalled the verse in *parashas Eikev*:

> [Eretz Yisrael is a] land which Hashem, your God, looks after constantly; the eyes of God [*einei Hashem*] are always upon it, from the beginning of the year until the end of the year.
>
> DEVARIM 11:12

As Rashi explains: "Hashem looks after all the other lands in the world... but it is through the attention [which Eretz Yisrael receives] that the rest of the world benefits."

Perhaps because of this special relationship which Hashem has with Eretz Yisrael, our Sages, of blessed memory, have declared: A person should always [choose to] live in Eretz Yisrael, even in a city which is inhabited by a majority of idolaters, rather than to live in the Diaspora, even in a city which is inhabited by a majority of Jews. Whoever lives in Eretz Yisrael is like someone who believes in God, and whoever lives in the Diaspora is like someone who does not believe in God" (*Kesubbos* 110b).

Anyone, therefore, who is looking to discover *hashgachah pratis* in the world, will have an especially easy time in Eretz Yisrael. Even if you spend as little as one day there — not a hundred years ago but even today — you can feel the gentle tap of *hashgachah pratis* on your shoulder. It is there that even an average person, such as myself, can gather enough anecdotal gems to fill the pages of a book.

The stories presented here are all true. Some of them are autobiographical. Others were told to me by eyewitnesses or by people who had heard them from eyewitnesses. In some cases, the stories were further corroborated by newspaper accounts. In all cases, the events are related here exactly as they were told or happened to me. While no details were changed other than names and identifying information in some of the stories, editorial license was utilized to add details of dialogue and description which make the stories more readable.

In selecting stories for this book, three major criteria were used. First, I wanted only "contemporary" stories, those which took place within the last twenty years. Second, I included only events which happened to ordinary people, like you and me, to emphasize the point that *hashgachah pratis* is not reserved only for famous Rabbis or outstanding Torah scholars. And third, I chose only anecdotes which occurred in Eretz Yisrael, to underscore the fact that Eretz Yisrael merits the uniquely intimate watch of *Einei Hashem* more than any other place on earth.

One of the appellations for Hashem is *Ha-Makom*, literally, "the place," emphasizing the fact that His Providence can be felt in any corner of the world. Nevertheless, just as a mother's love can span the oceans but is felt more intimately at home, so too, the *hashgachah pratis* of Hashem fills the world but is experienced more intensely in the only land referred to by Jews as "holy."

It is my fervent hope that these stories will increase awareness of the extent to which *hashgachah pratis* guides our daily lives, wherever we live. Perhaps you will be encouraged to begin keeping your own personal diary of miracles you have witnessed or heard from others.

If you do start such a journal, it will strengthen your own *emunah* in *hashgachah pratis* and help you strengthen the *emunah* of your friends, family, and any "not-yet-observant" Jews you meet. And when that happens, it will further prove how my seeing that announcement on a lamppost fifteen years ago was yet another example of *hashgachah pratis*.

Meir Wikler, D.S.W.
Brooklyn, New York

3

Introduction
"What is hashgachah pratis?"

A young man once approached the Chazon Ish, Rabbi Avraham Yeshaya Karelitz, *zatzal*, to ask a pedagogical question. This young Rabbi was about to assume the position of *mashgiach ruchani* (spiritual mentor) in a boys' Yeshivah high school. He wanted to know what moral points he should try to stress to the boys during his lectures. Which ethical principles should he emphasize?

The Chazon Ish replied that the *mashgiach* should focus on one point and one point alone: *hashgachah pratis.* "If the boys come away from your lectures with one lesson, it must be that the world is not *hefker* (abandoned, in no one's charge), that there is a Creator and nothing happens by chance! If you manage to teach this to your students, you will have achieved a great success. If you plant within them a deep appreciation for *hashgachah pratis*, their lives will be changed forever."

What is *hashgachah pratis*?

The Hebrew phrase, *hashgachah pratis*, is generally translated as "Divine Providence," but literally, it means "individualized supervision" from Hashem. It refers to the fundamental Jewish belief in the constant guiding hand of Heaven, which controls all Creation — from the orbits of the planets to the flight pattern of a mosquito.

As the Midrash (*Midrash Rabbah, Bereshis* 10:7) explains: "Rabbi Simon said, There is not even one blade of grass that does not have its own *mazal* in Heaven that taps it and says: Grow!" And the Talmud states that every living creature, "from the massive ox to the tiny flea, is directly sustained by the support decreed for it in Heaven" (*Avodah Zarah* 3b).

Hashgachah pratis means that Hashem notices, cares, and pays attention to all creatures. If this is true for plants and animals, it is even more so for human beings. Although events in our lives may be masked as "natural," *hashgachah pratis* means that everything that happens to us is Hashem's Will. As Rabbi Chanina declared, "A person does not prick his finger below [on earth] unless it is decreed for him above [in Heaven], as it is stated [*Tehillim* 37:23], 'A man's footsteps are established by Hashem' (*Chullin* 6b).

Rabbi Eliyahu Eliezer Dessler explains how even seemingly natural events are really acts of Heaven. He points out that with minimal effort we can all recognize the miracles of daily life:

> Even someone on the lowest [spiritual] level, someone to whom it appears that all events are 'natural,' if he will simply desire to think into the matter honestly, he will see that everything happens with direct guidance — that Hashem guides all 'natural' events.
>
> In order to understand how all natural events are really miracles, consider the following metaphor. A man is standing behind a curtain and is peeking into a room through a tiny hole. He sees a pen writing but he does not see the man who is writing with the pen. [Nevertheless, he knows that a man must be there, guiding the pen to write.] In a similar vein, the one whose eyes are closed and sees only 'natural' events does not understand that Hashem is at work. All 'natural' events are being directed by Hashem. Just as the pen does not write by itself, so too, events in this world do not happen by themselves.
>
> MICHTAV ME-ELIYAHU, VOL. 3, p.164*

Rambam cites belief in *hashgachah pratis* as the first of his thirteen principles of faith which constitute the basis of Judaism. These principles are listed in many *siddurim* at the

---

* Feldheim, 1989.

end of *Shacharis*, the morning service, and they are recited by many at the conclusion of their prayers:

I believe with perfect faith that the Creator, blessed be His Name, creates and guides all creatures; and that He alone caused, causes, and will cause everything that happens.

Why did Maimonides and the Chazon Ish place such a primary emphasis on *hashgachah pratis*? Why is this principle so important?

Perhaps we can understand this with the insight offered by Rashi, in his commentary on the Torah verse which commands us to remember how Amalek attacked the Jews after the Exodus from Mitzrayim (*Devarim* 25:17). The Torah further commands us to destroy the very memory of Amalek.

Why is this enemy of the Jews singled out for total annihilation? Weren't there other nations who also attacked the Jews? What was so terrible about Amalek?

The Torah commands us to remember Amalek and, "what happened to you on the way." Rashi emphasizes that the Hebrew word "happened" is similar to the word "happenstance." In other words, Rashi lists as the first of his three interpretations of this phrase, that Amalek's wickedness was rooted in their attitude of happenstance — as if the Exodus had *occurred*, and did not result from Providence; as if the Jews were freed from slavery because of geopolitical forces and not Divine intervention; and as if the Red Sea "coincidentally" split just when the Jews needed to go through, and was not a miraculous event.

According to Rashi's commentary, we can now understand why Amalek was singled out for total destruction. The attitude that events in this world are happenstance or coincidence is diametrically opposed to all that Judaism stands for. It is an attitude which contradicts everything that Jews believe. It is an attitude which the Torah declares cannot coexist with the Jewish people's fulfillment of their mission in this world.

Throughout the history of the Jewish people, the greatest ideological threats have come from the "ism"s which espoused philosophies antithetical to the principle of *hashgachah pratis*. On the other hand, in ghettos and concentration camps the greatest inspiration that kept Jews alive both physically and spiritually was the unshakable belief in *hashgachah pratis*.

Especially now, as we hear Mashiach's approaching footsteps, let us reaffirm our belief in *hashgachah pratis*, as we witness its impact on our daily lives.

The Kiosk Speaks

Glancing past my cousin's shoulder and through his living room window, I can see the red ball of the August sun setting over the hills of Yerushalayim. It is magnificent and riveting. My mind has drifted from our conversation and does not reconnect until I hear the key words, "*hashgachah pratis.*"

"...so if you really want to hear a unique story of *hashgachah pratis*, Meir, you should go to that kiosk," my cousin, Yaakov, advises after learning that I am on the lookout for unusual examples of Divine Providence in Israel.

"I'm sorry, Yanky. My mind must have wandered. Which kiosk? What story?"

Yaakov fills me in on the details as he understands them. Then he suggests, "But why don't you go and speak with the proprietor yourself? That way you'll be sure you're getting the story accurately, without any exaggeration."

So I do, the very next day.

✧   ✧   ✧

Kiosks are a familiar part of the Israeli urban landscape. Small, light structures which serve as refreshment stands, they sell soft drinks, rolls, sandwiches, a variety of snacks, cigarettes, and also newspapers.

The kiosk which Yaakov mentioned is located across from the national convention center, Binyanei ha-Umah, in the area of the central bus station. The kiosk is not exactly at a place one would go to as a destination, but it is a much-frequented transfer point for hundreds of bus travelers.

Not knowing exactly what to expect, I approach the kiosk with some reservations. Maybe this isn't the one that my cousin Yaakov had in mind? Will the proprietor of the kiosk have time to speak with me? What if he's unfriendly or uncooperative?

The kiosk appears new and is painted a bright blue. A large blue canopy crowns the modest structure. Across the top are the Hebrew words *Pitzutz shel Kiosk* — an "explosion" of a kiosk — a play on words, the full meaning of which becomes clear to me only after I speak with the proprietor.

I wait until he finishes serving all of his customers. "Excuse me," I begin in my best Hebrew. "Shalom. My name is Meir. Someone told me that you were saved from a terrorist bomb that..."

Before I have a chance to finish my sentence, I am interrupted by a thirsty traveler who has just run up to the kiosk. "Please, one Coke. My bus is coming right now."

Again, I introduce myself. Now that he is not so busy he is most willing to talk with me.

A tall, athletic looking man in his middle thirties, wearing a colored T-shirt and a knitted yarmulka, he nods and introduces himself. "My name is David. Nice to meet you."

Before I have a chance to explain *why* I want to hear about the terrorist bomb, he reaches for a plastic food storage container on a shelf inside the kiosk. It contains photographs. He takes out the pile and begins to explain them, one at a time. This is obviously not the first time he has done so.

"Here — this was taken shortly after the explosion."

I look back and forth between the picture and the kiosk trying to visualize the scene. In order to help me, David steps out of his kiosk and onto the street, holding the picture up. "You see the lamppost in the picture? That's this one here. And you see this tree? That's the tree over there."

It is quite clear to me now that I am standing on the exact spot where the bomb exploded. David continues his recreation of the scene by holding up another picture of the same spot from a slightly different angle. "You see this dead man lying on the ground? That was the terrorist. He was the only one killed. There were no other casualties, *baruch Hashem*."

I feel my mouth become dry as the impact of David's words sink in. He holds up a third picture and continues. "You see this rubble over here? That's all that was left of my kiosk! It absorbed the full intensity of the explosion. The kiosk you see today is brand new."

David returns to his kiosk to serve the small line of customers that has formed while he was standing with me near the curb. He is doing a brisk business selling drinks now, in the midday heat. Some customers buy candies or snacks to go with their drinks.

After everyone is served, David calls me to the narrow doorway at the side of the kiosk. He hands me a small, hardcover edition of *Tehillim* and asks me to open it. Inside the cover, scrawled in pencil, is the date, "25/12/94" (December 25, 1994). "That was the date of the terrorist attack," David explains. "The *Tehillim* and this *mezuzah* were all that were salvageable from my kiosk. I found them in the rubble. You saw the pictures. Nothing else remained — nothing."

David turns to serve more customers. He patiently waits as a mother tries to prod her son to make up his mind between a soft drink and an ice-cream bar. The boy finally decides on the drink. His mother pays. David gives her the change. No, her son reconsidered and now wants the ice cream. His mother makes up the difference. David patiently exchanges the drink for an ice-cream bar and then returns to me.

"Was anyone hurt?" I ask gingerly.

"Yes. Fourteen people. All were waiting for a bus. But none of the injuries were serious, *baruch Hashem*. Let me explain why."

David steps outside and points to the bus stop just a few feet from his kiosk. "People were standing over there, waiting for the bus."

He turns halfway around and points in the opposite direction. "The bomb exploded over there, where we were standing before. My kiosk was right between the bomb and the bus stop, so it absorbed the full impact of the blast and actually shielded the travelers."

By now, my mouth is so dry I also need a drink. I buy one from David.

The *hashgachah pratis* is amazing, I think to myself. Only the *Tehillim* and *mezuzah* survived the blast! The kiosk protected the travelers! Only the terrorist was killed by his own bomb!

David has a satisfied look on his face as he watches me shake my head in disbelief. He has told this story many times before, I conclude to myself.

Now the obvious question occurs to me and I am almost afraid to ask. But I have come this far; I might as well pursue the story all the way. "Uh, tell me, David... where were *you* when this happened?"

"I was at home. I heard about it on the radio. At first I thought that the bomb had exploded across the street, over there. The announcer said, 'in front of *Binyanei ha-Umah*,' so I thought they meant my friend's kiosk across the street. It wasn't until I got to work that I discovered my own kiosk had been blown up."

"When did this happen?"

"At exactly 6:20 in the morning." David then volunteers the significance of the timing. "You see, it was early on a Sunday morning. The terrorist chose this spot because every Sunday morning dozens of soldiers gather here to catch army buses back to their bases after their Shabbat leave.

"The suicide bomber was dressed in an Israeli army uniform, disguised as a soldier. He tried to get on the bus but the bus driver pulled away before the bomb went off. It exploded as the bus drove off and only the rear window of the bus was shattered. None of the soldiers on the bus were hurt at all, *baruch Hashem*."

I nod in agreement.

"And what time do you usually open your kiosk on Sundays?"

David smiles at my question. He knows what is coming. "Generally, I open up at 7:30. That's when people begin to gather here to wait for buses on their way to work. I'm never here at 6:20. But just the week before, my friend who owns the kiosk across the street suggested to me that we open up at 6:00 on Sunday morning. He mentioned the soldiers' buses and said we could do a lot of business then.

"At first, I wasn't interested — another few shekels don't matter that much to me. But finally he convinced me that it would be worthwhile. So I agreed. And I planned, *just that day*, to open up at 6:00 instead of 7:30."

There is a long pause as I hesitate with my next question. "And why didn't you open up at 6:00, as you had planned?"

David stares ahead as if he is scanning the horizon for the answer. He slowly turns back to me and shakes his head. "I don't know. Honestly, I don't know."

I persist and rephrase my question. "But something must have delayed you or made you change your plans?"

David just smiles at me. "As I told you, I had every intention of opening up at 6:00 that Sunday morning. I even got up on time. But somehow, I just didn't go. I can't even explain it to myself. It wasn't as if there was something specific that I could point to as the reason. I just didn't go, and was still at home when the first reports came over the radio."

I stubbornly try one more time. "David, there must have been something that you thought about or that you got involved with that delayed you. *Something* must have kept you back that morning. What was it?"

David smiles again and does not answer. He just reaches up, brings down his book of *Tehillim* again, and points to it. We both begin to cry, silently.

> Behold, He does not slumber; He does not sleep, the protector of Yisrael... Hashem protects you from all evil; He protects your soul.
>
> TEHILLIM 121:4-7

[as heard from David Amuyal, Gilo, Jerusalem]

13

Happiness Is
a State of Mind

In 1987, Yeshivah Aish Hatorah decided to provide a public service by sponsoring a forum on "Happiness and How to Achieve It." Rabbi Zelig Pliskin, author of *Gateway to Happiness*,[*] was the featured speaker.

In order to attract primarily American tourists, the lecture was scheduled during the summer and held at the plush King David Hotel in Yerushalayim. The event was widely publicized and, due to the reputation of the speaker and the topic to be addressed, drew a standing-room-only crowd.

The theme of Rabbi Pliskin's address was based on his recently published book. Regardless of the circumstances surrounding any particular situation in life, he explained to the audience, a person is free to choose the attitude with which he will view that situation. If, for example, he chooses to adopt a positive perspective, he is capable of achieving happiness in almost any situation.

Rabbi Pliskin's own cheerful demeanor and upbeat presentation amplified his remarks and helped drive his point home. He liberally spiced his talk with anecdotes of various challenges in life which people met more easily because of their positive outlook. Before concluding his presentation, Rabbi Pliskin invited comments and questions from the audience.

Generally, Rabbi Pliskin looks forward to this part of the program. The question-and-answer period is an opportunity for him to get the feedback he values so highly. This is his

---

[*] Aish Hatorah Publications, 1983.

chance to interact with members of the audience and clarify points that may have been unclear.

The unexpected nature of the audience reaction is also appealing to Rabbi Pliskin. One never knows what is coming. Usually, Rabbi Pliskin enjoys that. This time, however, he wasn't so sure.

✧   ✧   ✧

At the conclusion of his speech, Rabbi Pliskin put down his notes. "Now I'd really like to hear from *you*. Some of you may have heard these ideas for the first time. What do you think about what I've said? How does all of this strike you? I'm always fascinated by the different reactions people have to these ideas and tonight I'd very much appreciate hearing yours. Please begin by introducing yourselves."

Sometimes there is a long pause after Rabbi Pliskin invites comments. People are either shy, awkward, or just uncomfortable about speaking up in public. Moreover, the size of the audience seems to affect their responsiveness; the larger the audience, the less likely they are to volunteer their questions and comments.

But that night, Rabbi Pliskin had barely finished speaking before a hand shot up, right in the middle of the well-filled hall.

A middle-aged, balding man with a southern accent stood up and removed a well-chewed cigar from his mouth. "My name is Steve, Rabbi," he began in a booming voice which exuded confidence and foreshadowed the confrontation to follow. "Your talk was very interesting and informative. I especially enjoyed the story you told about the Chofetz Chaim. I must say I have never heard that one before."

Steve gestured with his cigar and continued. "But honestly, Rabbi, do you really expect us to believe that a person can reframe *any* situation in a positive light? Come on, now. Certainly there are *some* situations in life that simply cannot be viewed positively. Wouldn't you agree?"

Not waiting for an answer, Steve delivered what he assumed to be the coup de grace. "For example, you could not find even one in a million who would have, say, uh... a flat tire on the highway and then feel good about it. I mean, who could feel good about a flat tire? Surely, even you would agree that a flat tire is nothing but a bummer. So not *every* situation can be 'reframed positively,' as you say."

During the brief pause that followed, Rabbi Pliskin thought about how to respond. What could he say that would be acceptable to Steve? What answer would satisfy him?

The hushed crowd anxiously waited for Rabbi Pliskin's response. As he stroked his red beard and glanced around the packed hall, suddenly another hand went up. Rabbi Pliskin decided to call on the man who was raising his hand, who just happened to be sitting next to Steve.

"Rabbi, my name is Alan and if it's all right with you, I'd like to answer Steve's question."

"Uh... sure. Go right ahead," Rabbi Pliskin said encouragingly.

Alan stood up hesitantly. He seemed slightly uncomfortable about speaking publicly and lacked Steve's bold self-confidence. He looked about Steve's age or a bit older and he wore a pair of reading glasses on a thin, gold chain around his neck.

"A couple of years ago, I had a serious heart condition," Alan began. "I had severe chest pains for about two weeks before I went to my doctor. I put off making an appointment because I was too scared to find out what was wrong.

"After the examination, my doctor told me that if I wanted to see my next birthday, I had to radically alter my lifestyle. I had to quit smoking immediately. He put me on a strict low-fat, salt-free diet and I had to cut back from my twelve-hour days at my law firm. I couldn't use the subway or drive in rush-hour traffic, and I wasn't allowed to do any exercise or even lift a suitcase.

"Believe me, Rabbi, I was scared, so I followed my doctor's orders religiously. I kept regular appointments with him and never cheated on the diet. I've known my doctor for over twenty years and he never exaggerates. I knew that if he insisted on

16

such drastic measures, then my life depended on them.

"After twelve months, the doctor himself could not believe the recovery I had made. He was so pleased that he told me I was no longer in danger. He said he hoped I would not resume smoking or go back to being a workaholic, but I could return to normal activity.

"I was so excited, I was afraid that I wasn't hearing him correctly. So I asked him to be more specific.

"'Alan,' he said. 'You can do any exercise you want now. You can lift whatever you like. Anything. You can even...oh, change a flat tire, if necessary. Your electrocardiogram is excellent.'

"I floated home that night on cloud nine. I was so relieved. My wife and I went out to dinner the next night to celebrate. I felt as if I had been given a new lease on life. I was so grateful I cannot begin to describe it.

"Two days later, I was driving to work in the middle of a thunderstorm, and I suddenly heard a loud hissing noise. I pulled off the highway and reluctantly got out of my car to see what was wrong. I had a flat tire! As I opened the trunk to get out the jack and spare tire, I burst into tears — tears of euphoria. It suddenly hit me: I was about to change a flat tire, something I'd been forbidden to do all year, and something which now meant that I was well. I just stood there in the pouring rain alongside the highway crying like a baby. I was overwhelmingly grateful to have made such a complete recovery and to be able to demonstrate it to myself by changing a flat tire."

Alan sat down and took a deep breath.

Steve sat speechless, together with the entire audience.

Rabbi Pliskin was very moved by what he had just heard. He publicly thanked Alan for his invaluable contribution, answered some more questions, and adjourned the forum.

"What unbelievable *hashgachah pratis,*" Rabbi Pliskin observes today. "It would be absolutely mind-boggling to try to calculate the statistical probability of someone challenging me like Steve did and then finding someone else in the audience with Alan's experience. Less than one in a million, I'm sure.

"My message was driven home much better than if I'd answered Steve myself. Steve learned a lot about positive reframing from Alan's story, and so did I...and I hope that the rest of the audience benefited from it as well."

Then with a twinkle in his eye, Rabbi Pliskin adds, "And don't forget that Alan was sitting in the *same* row, *right next to* Steve. For me, that emphasizes the *hashgachah pratis* even more."

[*as heard from: Rabbi Zelig Pliskin,*
Kiryat Mattersdorf, Yerushalayim]

An Emergency Call

Bnei Brak is a middle-sized city with a population roughly equal to Afula in the north or Beersheva in the south. In spite of its size, however, this town, with its largely religious population, does not have a large police station. A single policeman on duty suffices. The crime rate among the residents of Bnei Brak is so low that police would simply be superfluous.

Although the residents of Bnei Brak do not need a large police force, they still need an emergency ambulance service. In Bnei Brak, as in many religious communities in Israel, a volunteer ambulance service called Hatzalah augments the government ambulance service, Magen David Adom. Hatzalah members are all professionally trained volunteers. Most of the time these volunteers work at other jobs, but twenty-four hours a day they are on call in case of a medical emergency.

One of the Hatzalah members in Bnei Brak is Yossi Lieber.* A plumber by trade, Yossi is always on the go. If not for his beeper, even his wife would have a hard time reaching him. In order to be available for emergency medical calls, however, Yossi also carries a walkie-talkie so that the Hatzalah dispatcher will never have to wait even for a second. When a life is hanging in the balance, every second counts.

Since a skilled, reliable plumber can be hard to find, Yossi has more jobs than he can handle. Good-hearted as he is, he finds it hard to say no to anyone who desperately needs repairs. And because most plumbing jobs are urgent, Yossi seems to always be at least one job behind schedule.

---

* All of the names in this story have been changed by request.

In spite of his heavy workload, though, Yossi never loses his composure or his sense of priorities. "No matter how bad the leak," Yossi often says, "it is never as serious as the loss of even one drop of Jewish blood." So when his walkie-talkie crackles, he drops everything and runs to his ambulance.

✧ ✧ ✧

It was a warm Spring day shortly after Pesach when Yossi had just finished installing a rooftop solar water heater. He was walking toward his van, an hour late for his next appointment, when he stopped to catch his breath.

Adjusting his plumber's cap, Yossi happened to glance down, and he noticed an unusually large envelope on the sidewalk. As Israelis have to be wary of suspicious objects, Yossi neither ignored it nor picked it up.

A strong breeze came up and blew the envelope easily along the sidewalk. Yossi was relieved. If the envelope was light, it was not a bomb, he thought. But his curiosity was piqued, so he picked up the envelope and looked inside.

Yossi had seen some unexpected sights in his life, but never had he seen such a large amount of money at one time. His knees began to buckle as he stared at what looked like an endless wad of cash.

Yossi jumped inside his van and counted the money. When he finished, he could not believe that he was in possession of the astronomical sum of 300,000 shekels, all in large bills. I have to find the owner and return this money, he thought. But how? There was no identification on the envelope.

Yossi was so overwhelmed that he completely forgot about his next appointment. But he never forgot his commitment to save lives, so when his walkie-talkie crackled at that moment, it took him away from his dilemma. He reached for the walkie-talkie and turned up the volume.

"A man collapsed at home. Could be a heart attack. Yossi, are you available to take the call?"

"Give me the address already," Yossi barked into his

walkie-talkie as he sped to his ambulance, still clutching the envelope. The money will just have to wait, he told himself.

Yossi knows the streets of Bnei Brak better than a cab driver does. He switched on the siren, found the address easily and was banging on the door so soon after the call came in that the family was surprised to see him.

"Where is he?" Yossi demanded as he raced into the third-floor apartment of Shlomo Ashkenazi.

"Here! Here!" replied a frantic, pale Mrs. Ashkenazi.

Inside the modest bedroom, Shlomo was lying on the floor, unconscious.

Yossi flung his medical bag on the floor and got right to work. First he checked Shlomo's pulse and breathing. *Baruch Hashem*, he's still alive, Yossi thought. Next, he loosened Shlomo's belt and tie. Then he reached for a syringe and gave Shlomo an injection.

Yossi was working so quickly that he seemed to be doing two things at the same time. Shlomo's wife and children stood huddled in the doorway saying *Tehillim*, afraid to step in and afraid to walk out. Yossi seemed to know what to do so well that the Ashkenazi family was filled with hope.

Yossi was checking vital signs, vigorously massaging Shlomo's chest and administering medication, all at the same time. I've never lost one yet and I don't plan to break my record now, he told himself. "Come on, come on..." Yossi coaxed, as he felt Shlomo's pulse rate increase. "That's it, that's it."

For the first time since he'd entered the Ashkenazi apartment, Yossi let himself relax for a moment. He dropped his tired arms and took a deep breath. Then he leaned over Shlomo and watched eagerly as Shlomo's eyelids fluttered open. Upon regaining consciousness, Shlomo tried to sit up. But Yossi stopped him.

"Not so fast, young man," Yossi said firmly, stopping him. Then, over his shoulder he added, "Looks like he'll be all right, *baruch Hashem*."

One trembling wife and five children echoed, softly, "*Baruch Hashem*."

The atmosphere in the Ashkenazi home had been tense

and fearful when Yossi had dashed in a few minutes earlier. Now the joy of relief and hopefulness was almost tangible.

Suddenly Yossi shouted, "Oh, no!" Shlomo had passed out again.

Instinctively, Mrs. Ashkenazi pulled her children back to give Yossi more room to work. Once again, Yossi flew into action. More massaging. More *Tehillim* from Mrs. Ashkenazi. More whimpering from the children.

"Tell me," Yossi asked, "has this ever happened before? Does he have a heart condition that you know of?"

"No, *never*," she replied desperately, as if her emphasis would help her husband.

"I may need to call for back-up on this one," Yossi said to himself as he continued to try to revive Shlomo.

Gradually, Yossi relaxed — and then once again he received the reward he had been waiting for: Shlomo opened his eyes.

"*Baruch Hashem!*" was sighed first by Yossi and then echoed by Mrs. Ashkenazi and the children.

"Don't try to sit up yet," Yossi told him in a soothing tone. "Let's first make sure that you're all right and that you don't..."

Yossi stopped abruptly, gasped, and then swung into action again. He repeated the same procedures which had succeeded the first two times in reviving Shlomo. Without turning away from Shlomo, Yossi desperately called over his shoulder to Mrs. Ashkenazi. "Do you have any clue as to what may have brought this on?"

Mrs. Ashkenazi remained frozen behind Yossi and surrounded by her terrified children. She groped for answers to assist this stranger who was trying to save her husband's life.

"Well, he...he did suffer a terrible shock shortly before he passed out," Mrs. Ashkenazi said.

"Do you mean an electrical shock?" Yossi cried.

"No, no... an emotional shock," Mrs. Ashkenazi replied quickly.

"What kind of emotional shock? What happened?"

"Shlomo had just returned from a business meeting," she explained. "As he was taking off his jacket, he realized that he had lost an envelope that contained 300,000 shekels...."

Yossi Lieber succeeded in reviving his patient one more time. When Shlomo regained consciousness, Yossi quickly informed him that the lost envelope was found. After Shlomo had absorbed the amazing news, Yossi retrieved the envelope from his jacket and handed it to Shlomo.

All of Shlomo's vital signs then returned to normal. No further medical treatment was necessary. *Baruch Hashem*.

[as heard from Zelig Dolinsky, Kiryat Mattersdorf, Jerusalem, and reported in Chadashot Mishpachah, August 10, '95]

Finding a
New Home

A few years ago, Rabbi Leizer Feinberg* was one of the youngest
teachers on the staff of Yeshivah Torah Ore, in the Mattersdorf
section of Yerushalayim. Rabbi Feinberg sports a short,
auburn beard, which contributes to his youthful and cheerful
appearance. He dresses appropriately for his position, in a
black suit, opened-neck white shirt, and black fedora. But the
lilt in his voice, the twinkle in his eye, and the beat-up, antique
Volvo that he drives all hint at a more colorful personality
beneath the dark attire.

As one might suspect, Rabbi Feinberg has not always worn
the uniform of a *maggid shiur* (Torah lecturer). Before his
marriage, Leizer (he prefers I drop the "Rabbi") was studying
in a Yeshivah whose style of dress was "more white than
black," to use his words. In other words, he wore a white,
knitted *kippah* on his head and no dark jacket over his white
shirt.

Both Leizer and his wife, Shoshana, come from American
families who immigrated to Israel when their children were
young. Thus they both consider themselves more Israeli than
American, although neither speaks English with an Israeli
accent.

When Leizer and Shoshana got married, they agreed that
Leizer should continue learning Torah in *kollel*, "for a year or
two." They both expected that eventually Leizer would leave
his full-time Yeshivah studies. Nevertheless, they felt that they

---

* All of the names in this story have been changed by request.

24

wanted to begin their married life together on the foundation of a *kollel* lifestyle.

The *kollel* lifestyle was a slight departure from that of their parents. Although neither set of parents objected, nevertheless adopting a *kollel* lifestyle did require a conscious, deliberate decision on their part. In keeping with this "shift to the right," as Leizer puts it, he decided to look for another Yeshivah which would complement his new outlook.

Without much fanfare and upon the advice of his *rebbeim*, he decided on Yeshivah Torah Ore. There Leizer found a good mix of Americans and Israelis. The level of learning was advanced and challenging, and the atmosphere was tolerant enough to accommodate someone coming from a more modern Yeshivah without making him feel uncomfortable or out of place. At the same time, Torah Ore was very much a mainstream "black" Yeshivah (i.e., black suits, black hats, etc.).

At the time that Leizer entered the *kollel* of Torah Ore, he and Shoshana were living in a settlement of modern Orthodox Jews, a twenty-minute drive from Yerushalayim. Shoshana and Leizer felt very much at home there at the beginning. Leizer especially enjoyed spending his weeks in the "yeshivish" atmosphere of Kiryat Mattersdorf and his weekends in his *yishuv*. He felt he had found the perfect balance, enabling him to maintain his "middle-of-the-road" outlook.

After about two years, the Feinbergs began to think about moving to Yerushalayim. Although they loved their *yishuv*, by now the friends they felt closest to lived in Yerushalayim. Moreover, they had begun to feel a little out of place there and they longed for a "more yeshivish community" in which to raise their young son.

The most obvious choice would be moving to Kiryat Mattersdorf in Yerushalayim, where Leizer's Yeshivah was located. But even though he had been learning there for quite a while, they had never once spent Shabbos in Mattersdorf. They weren't sure how they would feel. Was it really for them? Would they be comfortable there?

The only way to find out was to "test drive the neighborhood," as Leizer put it. So they made arrangements to spend a Shabbos in Mattersdorf as the guests of another *kollel* couple from Torah Ore.

Even before that Shabbos was over, Leizer and Shoshana knew that this was where they wanted to live. And by Saturday night they were already daydreaming out loud to each other about "some day living in Mattersdorf."

The Feinbergs' wish was more dream than reality for one very practical reason: they simply could not afford it.

The Feinbergs owned their modest apartment. This enabled them to make ends meet on the limited budget of Leizer's *kollel* check and Shoshana's part-time teaching job. All of their savings from before they got married and their monetary wedding presents were sunk into the down payment on their apartment so they certainly could not afford to buy another apartment in Mattersdorf. The real estate market at the time was such that selling their apartment was not a realistic option, either, and the rents were too high for the scarce rental apartments that were available in Mattersdorf. So Leizer and Shoshana resigned themselves to the fact that moving would be something they could wish for but never have.

That year Purim fell on a Friday. Just about everywhere in the world that means only that the normal holiday festivities in the afternoon must be curtailed somewhat. When Purim falls on any other day of the week, the celebration usually extends into the late afternoon and evening. But when Purim comes out on a Friday, the sanctity of Shabbos requires an early conclusion to the Purim merrymaking.

In the holy city of Yerushalayim, however, when Purim comes out on a Friday, it provides the special opportunity called *Purim meshulash* — or "triple Purim." On Friday, the *Megillah* is read and *tzedakah* is distributed, as in all other Jewish communities. On Shabbos, the *al ha-nissim* prayers are recited, because Yerushalayim celebrates Shushan Purim (the *Megillah* is not read then, however, as it is not read on Shabbos). And the Purim *seudah* and sending of *mishlo'ach manos* take place on Sunday.

Purim is a joyful holiday that is eagerly anticipated in every Jewish community. But in Yerushalayim, there is an added measure of excitement whenever the residents await a *Purim meshulash*.

That year was a *Purim meshulash* and the Feinbergs made arrangements to spend the special weekend in Yerushalayim. The three days of festivities was something the Feinbergs had never experienced before. Of course they knew all about *Purim meshulash*, but experiencing it was another matter entirely.

Thursday night and Friday all of the synagogues were packed for the reading of the *Megillah*. The levity of Purim spilled over and permeated the entire Shabbos that followed. And then on Sunday, the celebration literally exploded onto the very streets of this otherwise sleepy neighborhood.

Children and adults in the most creative and humorous costumes filled the streets, many carrying *mishlo'ach manos* to friends and neighbors. Music mingled with laughter in the street, creating a truly joyful atmosphere.

In the car on the way home that night, Shoshana brought up her favorite topic. "On Shabbos I had a few minutes to relax and I picked up a book by Rabbi Avigdor Miller," she told Leizer. "I just opened it at random and began reading — he was talking about how vital it is for the entire family to live in close proximity to a Yeshivah. I felt as if he were talking directly to us."

Leizer kept his eyes on the road, watching for the hairpin turns. "How did you know what was on my mind? But we already decided that we can't afford to move."

"I know," Shoshana countered. "But let's just talk again about what we would need and what we could afford. You never know."

"Well, I suppose now, with the new baby, we'd need at least a two-bedroom apartment. And we couldn't possibly manage a rent of anything higher than $500 a month, but we're never going to find that."

"Maybe not, but there's no harm in trying. Why don't you speak with Reb Nochum tomorrow? Who knows?"

The next day, Leizer approached Reb Nochum, an older friend from another *kollel* in Yerushalayim who dabbled in apartment rentals on the side, and asked if he knew of any two-bedroom apartments for rent in Mattersdorf for around $500 a month.

"Are you kidding?" replied Reb Nochum. "I'd love to help you find a place, but there's no way you're going to find anything for that price."

Not really expecting a different reply, Leizer was not disappointed. He shared Reb Nochum's words with Shoshana later that evening and that was that.

The following morning, as Leizer entered the Yeshivah, he could not believe his eyes. There on the bulletin board in Torah Ore was a small handwritten sign that read: "Two-bedroom apartment in Mattersdorf, $500/month, ACT FAST," followed by a phone number. Leizer couldn't wait to get to a phone.

The man who answered turned out to be an apartment broker who learned in the mornings at Torah Ore — and sat at the other end of the *same bench* as Leizer! The apartment sounded too good to be true. But there was only one problem: the Feinbergs did not have even the $500 needed in advance for the first month's rent. In addition, they had no money for moving expenses. Nevertheless, Leizer told the broker he was very interested and would get back to him at the beginning of the following week.

"I'll hold it for you until then," the broker promised, "but no longer. An apartment for that price is hard to come by, you know."

"Where on earth are we going to come up with $500?" Shoshana asked.

"I haven't the faintest idea," Leizer replied sadly. "But I just couldn't bring myself to say, 'Thanks, but no thanks.'"

That Shabbos the Feinbergs were scheduled to visit with Shoshana's parents in the Yerushalayim neighborhood of Gilo. During the car ride, Leizer and Shoshana tried unsuccessfully to figure out a way to come up with the money they needed. As they approached Gilo, Leizer came to the inevitable conclusion. "I suppose Hashem just wants us to stay where we are."

When they arrived and unpacked that Friday afternoon, Shoshana found an envelope on her bed with her name on it. "What's this, Mom?" she asked.

"It's from your Uncle Moshe," her mother replied happily. "He heard you were coming for Shabbos and dropped it off last night. He said something about not having given you anything yet for the new baby."

Shoshana opened the envelope. Her eyes filled with tears when she found herself staring at a check for $750!

The Feinbergs realized that the unexpected gift was not only a sign from Heaven that they should, in fact, take the apartment in Mattersdorf, but was also a sign that they would be helped over the other hurdles that lay ahead, as well.

They used $500 for the first month's rent and the rest for moving expenses. They then immediately put their apartment up for sale and hoped for the best.

Their neighbors were amazed and concerned for their "crazy" friends. "How on earth could you give up your security and sell your home only to throw away the money on a rental?" they asked. Nevertheless, the Feinbergs were determined and carried out their plans to move to Mattersdorf.

The days turned into weeks and soon the Feinbergs' second month's rent was due. With no available cash and a strong distaste for borrowing beyond their means, they decided to take their apartment off the market for sale and try to rent it for $500 a month. They hung up signs around the *yishuv*, as well as in Yerushalayim, all with no success.

Finally, *the day before* their second month's rent was due, someone called to rent their apartment. Unfortunately, the prospective tenant explained, he was interested only in renting for one month until his own new apartment would be finished. The apartment should have been completed already, but such delays are not unusual in Israel where political events can have a direct impact on the building industry by cutting off the supply of Arab construction workers.

The Feinbergs would have preferred to rent their apartment on a long-term basis, but with the rent due the next day they had no complaints! Meanwhile they continued to look for a long-term tenant.

By the end of the second month, they still had not found one. What would they do now?

One morning the Feinbergs received a call from the people renting their apartment. Their own apartment was still not ready, the tenants explained. Could they possibly stay for one more month? The Feinbergs happily agreed.

The following month the Feinbergs received the same call from their tenants, but this time the request was only for an additional week, as their new apartment would be ready any day. By the end of the week, the tenant was calling to extend his stay another week, which the Feinbergs gladly granted. This was repeated again at the end of the third week as well.

When the tenant finally did move out, the Feinbergs were in the same predicament as before.

Once again, *on the day the rent was due*, the Feinbergs received a call from a prospective tenant. This time the family was looking to rent the apartment *for a full year*. Now the Feinbergs knew their rent would be covered for at least twelve months.

Before that first year was up, Leizer and Shoshana met with the *Rosh Yeshivah*, Rabbi Chaim Pinchas Scheinberg, *shlita*, to discuss a wide range of personal and family issues. During the course of the meeting the subject of their apartment came up. Rabbi Scheinberg advised them to sell it.

"We've tried many times to do just that," Leizer explained. "There just seems to be no market for apartments there now."

"Yes, I know, but try again anyway. If you sell the apartment you'll have money to buy another one and you won't have to worry about how you'll come up with the rent each month."

The Feinbergs took Rabbi Sheinberg's advice, and they were quite surprised when they did find a buyer — immediately. "It was as if he had given us a blessing," Shoshana observed.

The sale went through and it enabled the Feinbergs to purchase an apartment, not in Mattersdorf but in a new "Yeshivah community" that was just being built. They have since moved in and love both their new apartment and the deeply religious atmosphere of their new neighborhood. It is also just on the outskirts of Yerushalayim, which enables Leizer to travel easily to Yeshivah Torah Ore where he has recently joined the faculty as a *maggid shiur*.

The Feinbergs are still grateful for their new home and community. Recently, Leizer and Shoshana beamed with pride when they found their son and his friend — a great-grandson of the late Rabbi Shlomo Zalman Aurbach, *zatzal* — playing "*bikkurim* (first fruits)." A laundry basket served as the make-believe *bikkurim* and a laundry hamper was the *mizbe'ach* (altar). They are grateful for the Hand of Hashem which they felt guiding and helping them through the decision to move, the search for an apartment to rent and then one to buy, and the delicate balancing act of financing it all.

But, perhaps, they are most grateful for the fortuitous timing of the sale of their apartment. That transaction took place barely three months prior to the public announcement of the signing of the Oslo Accords.

The Oslo Accords began the "peace process," designed to grant autonomy to the Arab population living in some parts of Judea and Samaria. As a result of this dramatic, unexpected political development, real estate values in the Jewish settlements in these areas dropped.

Had the Feinbergs not sold their apartment when they did, they may have still been juggling finances today and worrying about finding a new home.

[as heard from Rabbi Leizer Feinberg, Ramat Shlomo]

Grandmother's Grave

You know what the house is like before you leave for a visit to Israel — the phone almost rings itself off the wall; the doorbell doesn't stop; everyone you know has just one last-minute request, letter, or greeting to send along. In the midst of all this, you're trying to finish your packing, say good-bye, and make sure you haven't forgotten anything.

For most people, the hours before an international flight are marked by high anxiety, stress, and tension. But for Yerachmiel Milstein, a lecturer in Aish Hatorah's Discovery Program, a trip to Israel ruffles his feathers less than a subway ride to Manhattan. Sure there's commotion in his house. But he sails through the final countdown with aplomb.

✧　✧　✧

Is Yerachmiel still here?" Mrs. Stern[*] asked hopefully. Breathless, she had rushed over on that hot July afternoon.

"Sure," Channie, Yerachmiel's wife, replied laughing. "He hasn't even *thought* of leaving for the airport yet! Come on in."

"Do you think he could do me a really big favor?" Mrs. Stern went on, hesitantly. "I've just got to get this empty suitcase to my brother-in-law in Har Nof and I don't know anyone else who's going to Israel."

Yerachmiel overheard the conversation and chimed in. "Har Nof? That's exactly where I'll be staying! May I suggest that you allow me to chaperon your suitcase to Israel? I shall

---

[*] not her real name

guard it with my life." Yerachmiel leapt in front of the suitcase as if to protect it from imaginary attackers. "Get back, get back! I promised to guard this suitcase with my life and you shall not make me into a liar." .

"Oh, Yerachmiel!" Mrs. Stern caught her breath from laughing. "Would you really take it for me? It would be such a big favor. I just didn't know how on earth I was going to get this to Chaim, my brother-in-law."

"Now I know why I had to take this business trip," Yerachmiel quipped. "It was all part of the Divine plan to get this suitcase to your brother-in-law in Israel. I'm really glad to be able to help. Since I'm only going for a week, I just have one suitcase of my own — so you see, you're actually doing *me* a favor."

"I'm doing *you* a favor?"

"Sure. Now when I walk through the airport, I won't be lopsided, carrying only one suitcase."

"You're impossible!" Mrs. Stern laughed, and then asked, "Will you be taking care of business the entire week?"

"Oh, I might have one day free, if all goes well," Yerachmiel said. "And if I do," he went on, suddenly becoming serious, "I'd love to be able to visit my grandmother's *kever* in Cholon."

"And if you don't finish your packing," Channie added, "you'll only be visiting the airport."

In spite of all the delays, Yerachmiel made it to the airport in time. After take-off, he prepared for some of his upcoming meetings at the Yeshivah, and then sat back and reflected on the possibility of visiting his grandmother's grave.

Yerachmiel's grandmother, Rebbetzin Fayga Gnatt, *a"h*, was the daughter of Rabbi Yerachmiel Yaakov Gnatt, *zatzal*. Being able to visit her grave held special significance for Yerachmiel, who was named after Rabbi Gnatt, his great-grandfather. He had been unable to travel to Cholon on his most recent trips to Israel, which made him all the more eager to do so now.

The first three days of Aish Hatorah's international meeting were even more hectic than Yerachmiel had anticipated.

Nevertheless, he welcomed the opportunity to network with other Discovery faculty from around the world as well as recharge his spiritual batteries from the boundless source of energy which is Rabbi Noach Weinberg, *shlita*. In addition, Yerachmiel was enjoying the bonus of visiting with his brother, Yosef, and his family in Har Nof.

On the morning of the third day of Yerachmiel's visit, he was planning his visit to the cemetery when the doorbell rang at Yosef's apartment. It was Chaim Stern,* who came to pick up the empty suitcase his sister-in-law had sent with Yerachmiel. Chaim and Yerachmiel had never met but they quickly got acquainted.

"So what are your plans for today?" Chaim asked, after learning that Yerachmiel was in Israel for less than a week.

"I'm hoping to take care of a few things in the Tel Aviv area."

"No kidding? That's exactly where I'm headed now. I have to take this suitcase to my aunt in Ra'anana. My taxi is waiting for me right outside. Maybe you'd like to come along? I would enjoy a companion in the back seat and there's a place on the way where you could get off and catch a bus."

Yerachmiel wasn't planning to leave quite so early but he always liked to take advantage of unexpected opportunities. "Sure," he said. "Just let me grab my hat."

Chaim and Yerachmiel jumped into the waiting taxi and sped off.

About twenty minutes outside of Yerushalayim, Chaim noticed a gas station alongside the highway. Since he was quite thirsty, he asked the driver to stop.

"Once you leave the cool mountain air of Yerushalayim you really begin to feel the heat," Chaim commented to Yerachmiel. "Would you like something to drink?"

"No, thanks," Yerachmiel replied, climbing out of the taxi. "I'll just stretch my legs a bit."

Once outside the air-conditioned taxi, however, Yerach-

---

* not his real name

miel felt the impact of the strong July sun and changed his mind. Maybe I will buy a soda, he thought.

Yerachmiel entered the combination gas station/kiosk/variety store and found Chaim engrossed in a newspaper. As Yerachmiel was trying to decide what to buy, he reached for his wallet. Suddenly, his stomach bottomed out in the free-fall panic known by anyone who has ever forgotten his wallet at home. I knew there was something else I had to grab besides my hat, he moaned to himself.

"So, you changed your mind about the drink?" Chaim asked, looking up from the paper.

"No, I, uh, just wanted to keep you company," Yerachmiel bluffed, trying to keep his composure. He then pretended to look out of the window as his thoughts raced.

Yerachmiel helplessly pictured his wallet sitting on the night table in his bedroom in Har Nof. He didn't even have any small change in his pocket. He was, temporarily, penniless. He reviewed his options quickly.

He could ask Chaim to take him back to Yerushalayim. But that would delay Chaim by almost an hour. He just couldn't do that.

He could ask Chaim to loan him some money. But Yerachmiel would need enough money for bus fares around Tel Aviv and Cholon and back to Yerushalayim in the evening. He couldn't bring himself to ask someone he barely knew for money. Besides, he would be too embarrassed to admit that he had been so careless as to forget his wallet.

He could try to borrow money from someone he knew in Tel Aviv. But he had no money to *get* to Tel Aviv. And even if he got there, he couldn't be certain he would find anyone at home.

Getting back to Yerushalayim wasn't Yerachmiel's greatest concern at the moment — he had hitched rides in Israel before. What really upset him was that without any money, there was no way at all he could manage to visit his grandmother's grave in Cholon. As this was the only free day of his trip, that meant he would have to forfeit this most meaningful item on his agenda. And who knows how long it would be until he would be back in Israel again?

Waves of disappointment washed over Yerachmiel as he hid his shame and despair behind a false smile and reentered the taxi.

After some small talk about the oppressive heat that day, Chaim asked the last question Yerachmiel wanted to hear. "What are you planning to do today in Tel Aviv? Are you going sightseeing, or are you planning to visit friends or relatives?"

"Well, uh, not really either. I, uh, was planning to... visit my grandmother's *kever* in Cholon." Yerachmiel's voice trailed off as he thought about the visit which he obviously would not be making now.

Chaim sat up abruptly, as if the taxi had stopped short. "You are going to your grandmother's *kever*?" he echoed in a whisper.

"Yes," Yerachmiel replied, puzzled at Chaim's response.

"You're going to *daven* at your bubby's *kever*," Chaim repeated slowly, almost to himself. He turned his face towards the window. A few moments later he turned back to Yerachmiel with reddened eyes.

"Look, would you please do me a *tremendous* favor?" Chaim begged.

"Sure, what is it?" Yerachmiel asked, somewhat cautiously, wondering what on earth he was getting himself into.

Chaim took out his wallet and quickly removed a few bills. He urgently pressed them into Yerachmiel's palm and then closed both of his hands around Yerachmiel's.

Looking straight into Yerachmiel's now widened eyes, Chaim explained. "Here's three hundred shekels. I know you don't need the money. But please, let me sponsor your trip to your grandmother's *kever*. Take taxis wherever you have to go today... on me."

Yerachmiel couldn't respond. All he could do was gape at his surprise benefactor.

Chaim swallowed hard and continued. "My grandparents were all killed in the Holocaust. My parents' entire families were wiped out without a trace. How I envy you that you even *know* where your grandparents are buried!" Tears filled his eyes. "I will never have the *zechus* to *daven* at my grandparents' *kevarim*. If you will accept this money from me, then I might have a small share in the great mitzvah that you are doing today. Please — I realize you hardly know me. But it would mean so much to me if you would accept this money."

Yerachmiel was speechless. He barely managed to nod his head in agreement.

"Thank you," Chaim said. "Thank you so much."

A few minutes later, the taxi pulled over to the curb at a busy intersection. Chaim pointed straight ahead. "This is where you should get off. I'm continuing this way to Ra'anana. That's the road to Tel Aviv and Cholon. You'll have no difficulty getting a taxi from here. Thanks again and *poyl oys allas guts* — may you [through your prayers] achieve everything good. It was very nice meeting you."

Yerachmiel stepped out onto the sunbaked sidewalk and said good-bye to Chaim. As the taxi drove off, he looked up to Heaven with tears of joy filling his eyes and whispered, "*Baruch Hashem! Baruch Hashem!*"

[as heard from Rabbi Yerachmiel Milstein,
Brooklyn, New York]

The Missing Stones

It does sound like a lot of walking," I told my wife. "But everyone swears by his tours. Let's do the Old City with him tomorrow. It's only a half-day tour and we have nothing planned for the morning anyway."

Malka agreed. So the next day we found ourselves huffing and puffing to keep up with Rabbi Yom Tov Cohen,* as his walking tour wound through the narrow alleys of the Old City of Yerushalayim.

After we spent some time at the Kosel, Rabbi Cohen led us back across the plaza. At the foot of a long, wide staircase, directly opposite the Wall, Rabbi Cohen turned right and entered a round, cavernous tunnel, reminiscent of the London underground.

At the end of the tunnel, two Israeli soldiers, standing on guard next to a metal detector, exchanged greetings with Rabbi Cohen as we all filed through the security gate. Once on the other side of the gate, Rabbi Cohen guided his tour off to the side so that he could explain something to the group.

Rabbi Cohen adjusted his weatherworn, black fedora and gestured in a single sweeping motion. "Who can tell me what you see here?"

Someone from the back called out, "We're at a crossroads."

"That's true," Rabbi Cohen acknowledged, stroking his long, salt-and-pepper beard. "We are standing at a crossroads. As a matter of fact, it is one of the few in the Old City where

---

* This name was changed by request.

five streets meet at a single point. But what else is unusual about this spot? Can anyone tell me?"

When no one even tried to answer, Rabbi Cohen offered another clue. "Look up. Can anyone tell me what's missing?"

Someone else called out, "There's no *mezuzah* on any of the archways?"

Patiently, Rabbi Cohen stroked his beard, again, and smiled. "That's true. There are no *mezuzos* on any of these archways. But that is not at all unusual here because we are standing at the beginning of the Moslem Quarter of the Old City."

Rabbi Cohen cleared his throat and offered yet another hint. "Look straight up, above where we are standing. Does anyone see anything unusual here?"

A young Yeshivah boy, wearing a New York Yankees cap, piped up. "There are no stones."

"Exactly!" exclaimed Rabbi Cohen. "If you look all around, you'll see that the walls and ceiling are all made of stones, some of them hundreds of years old. This section of the Old City was not destroyed in 1948 like the Jewish Quarter was. But if you look directly above, you'll see that the archway is made of relatively new cement."

We all craned our necks upward to verify what Rabbi Cohen had just told us.

Rabbi Cohen motioned for us to move over to the side and out of the way of passersby. "Now if you'll all move over here, I'll explain to you why the stones are missing from the center of the archway and why they were replaced with cement."

Some of the members of the tour leaned against the wall. Others sat on the floor. Malka and I took drinks from our water bottles as we all got ready to hear what we had come to expect would be a long and intriguing story from our guide.

Rabbi Cohen began in the rapid speech of someone who has told the same story repeatedly but, nevertheless, without losing any of the enthusiasm of the very first time he told it.

"After the Six-Day War, the Arabs were so frightened of the Israelis that white flags flew over the rooftops of the Moslem Quarter for months. But the Arabs began a campaign of terror in the late sixties which, unfortunately, has continued until today.

"The strategy was always the same," our guide went on. "A time bomb would be hidden somewhere where it would do the most damage, killing many innocent civilians in an explosion.

"It was also during the late sixties that the crowds attending *Kabbalas Shabbos* services at the Kosel were the largest. Of course, if any of you come to the Kosel now on Friday night, you'll still see enormous crowds of people. But it's nothing compared to the crowds that gathered during the late sixties — the entire area in front of the Kosel was packed solid, from shoulder to shoulder.

"After services were completed, approximately half of the people leaving the Wall would stream through the tunnel we just came out of. So some Arab terrorist had the bright idea that this would be a perfect place to plant a bomb.

"Now you have to picture the scene over here every Friday night in those years, as literally thousands of Jewish men, women and children were walking down the street. For a terrorist, it was an ideal scenario.

"So one Thursday night, an Arab terrorist planted a time bomb above the light fixture hanging at the center of this archway. The bomb was positioned out of sight of all the pedestrians walking underneath. It was set to explode at the exact time when most people would be passing by on their way home from Friday night services."

Each member of the tour gasped in horror, imagining the terrifying scene of carnage. Rabbi Cohen paused to allow a young Arab boy leading a heavily laden donkey to pass by the group.

A middle-aged man with a video camera around his neck called out, "Rabbi Cohen, how many people were killed in that attack?"

"Do you really want to know?" Rabbi Cohen replied, baiting his audience. A few heads nodded, while the rest of us were numb and frozen still.

Rabbi Cohen drew himself up to his full height. Towering over the tour group, he appeared somewhat like a Biblical figure. Then he raised his bushy eyebrows and announced, "None... absolutely no Jews were killed, whatsoever."

The group sighed with relief, as if they were listening to a news broadcast of events happening that day.

Rabbi Cohen went on to explain. "Miraculous events are always disguised in natural occurrences. We believe that this terrible tragedy was averted only by the Master of the Universe. But just in case you are curious as to the means with which the Creator saved his people, I'll tell you exactly what happened.

"As most of you know, not all Jews pray at the same time. The custom among many of the *Sepharadim* is to complete the Friday night services before or shortly after sundown. The *Ashkenazim* generally conduct their services later and finish anywhere from half an hour to an hour after sundown.

"On any given Friday night, therefore, there are two main waves of people who flow through that tunnel. The first wave, that of the *Sepharadim*, reaches this spot about fifteen minutes after sundown. The second and much larger wave, that of the *Ashkenazim*, begins to come by about fifteen to twenty minutes later.

"Since the second wave is usually much larger than the first, the terrorist set his bomb to explode at the time when the largest throngs of *Ashkenazim* would be passing by this spot. So he checked the time when the crowd was thickest on Friday night and he set his bomb for the exact same time the following week.

"The terrorist used a very sophisticated timing device that could be set to the minute, hours ahead of time. The timing device worked perfectly. Only the terrorist forgot something very important.

"Since this took place in the Spring, the onset of Shabbos was approximately ten minutes later from one week to the next. So by setting his bomb to explode at the time when the heaviest crowds of *Ashkenazim* passed by the week before, he managed to detonate his bomb right in the middle of the brief period when few Jews come through here. And on that particular Friday night, there wasn't one Jew at this spot at the time. You see, the *Sepharadim* had already passed by and the *Ashkenazim* had not yet arrived."

"So then no one was hurt at all?" I asked in amazement.

"No, not exactly," replied Rabbi Cohen. "I said no *Jews* were killed by the bomb. As it happened, one older Arab woman was passing by at the time of the blast and was killed. And two Arab children were slightly wounded."

Rabbi Cohen raised his long arm, again, and pointed to the arch. "After the blast, the Israeli government was afraid that the ceiling might collapse and damage the nearby houses. So they quickly repaired the archway with cement.

"Now you know why the stones are missing here," he concluded.

Rabbi Cohen glanced at his watch and then announced, "Come on, everyone. We still have a few more stops and it's getting late. Please, everyone keep up with me so we don't lose any time."

As I passed back under the archway, I looked up again to remember how the repaired archway looked and to remember the story... Then with a shudder I quickened my pace to get away from that spot as soon as possible.

Malka turned to me. "Now you have another story for your book, Meir. What unbelievable *hashgachah pratis*! Can you imagine what would have happened if that Arab just had a Hebrew calendar with candle-lighting time? Hashem really takes care of us all the time, even when we don't realize it."

Praise Hashem, all nations; exalt Him, all people. For He has granted kindness to us and Hashem's truth endures forever, praise Hashem.

TEHILLIM 117

I once heard Harav Shlomo Brevda, *shlita,* ask: Why should the nations of the world praise Hashem for the kindness granted to Jews? Of course, *we* should praise Hashem. But why should other nations praise Him for the kindness He has shown to us?

Harav Brevda explained that there are times that other nations secretly plot against the Jews and Hashem saves us without our even realizing that we were saved. At such times it is only our enemies who can fully praise Hashem, because it is only they who really know what destruction they had planned which was thwarted only by *hashgachah pratis*.

[as heard from Rabbi Yom Tov Cohen,
Ezras Torah, Yerushalayim]

Around the Campfire

Yeshivos generally do not promote extracurricular activities. If this is so in America, it is even more so in Eretz Yisrael, where any activities other than learning are frowned upon. In keeping with this "Torah only" philosophy, some teachers try to take full advantage of holiday celebrations to give their students a well-deserved break for relaxation and recharging.

One such *mechanech* is Rabbi Mordechai Dolinsky, former *mashgiach ruchani* (dean of students) for the *talmidim* of Yeshivah Torah Ore in Yerushalayim. A firm believer in the "Torah only" philosophy, he energetically encourages his students to avoid any and all distractions from their learning. But when opportunities come along for the boys to enjoy a holiday celebration, Rabbi Dolinsky is one of the first to plan the arrangements.

A good example of this extracurricular programming is the lively *simchas beis ha-sho'evah* that Rabbi Dolinsky hosts in his *sukkah* every year. Refreshments abound, the music is live and the singing, interspersed with *divrei Torah*, goes on till the wee hours of the morning. Anyone who has ever attended a *simchas beis ha-sho'evah* hosted by Rabbi Dolinsky knows that nothing else can even come close.

Another example of Rabbi Dolinsky's extracurricular activities is the campfire he arranges every year on the night of Lag ba-Omer. While bonfires are a traditional custom throughout Eretz Yisrael, there are none that can compare with the unique atmosphere of Rabbi Dolinsky's campfires.

Refreshments are *de rigueur*. There is always live music and plenty of soulful singing. But that's not all. What would a campfire be without a story? So in his down-to-earth and homey style, Rabbi Dolinsky always prepares a story to tell around the campfire.

The stories Rabbi Dolinsky tells are always true and teach a moral lesson. The following story was told on the night of Lag ba-Omer, 1994, as the boys from Yeshivah Torah Ore sat around the campfire at the foot of one of the rolling hills behind Kiryat Mattersdorf.

✧   ✧   ✧

As *mashgiach*, Rabbi Dolinsky sees his role as more than just a teacher. He believes a good *mashgiach* must also serve, at times, as confidant, nurse, travel agent, medical referral, advisor, and even *shadchan* (matchmaker).

Not too long ago, Rabbi Dolinsky decided that two boys in particular needed extra assistance in finding their mates, so he decided to help with more than just advice and encouragement. He went over to the home of Rebbetzin Stein* who is very involved in matchmaking and asked for a suggestion for one of the boys. As it turned out, she came up with a candidate that seemed more suited to the other boy Rabbi Dolinsky had in mind, a twenty-one-year-old named Asher Laniado*.

Asher, an Israeli, was not that fluent in English. The girl who was recommended, Chana Shapiro*, was an American who was studying in Israel, and who was not too fluent in Hebrew. So far, it doesn't sound like much of a match, does it? But both Asher and Chana happened to be fluent in Spanish, which is one of the reasons why Rabbi Dolinsky thought that they might be compatible.

Asher's parents immigrated to Eretz Yisrael from Argentina before he was born. As they continued to speak Spanish at home, Asher became fluent in Spanish as well as Hebrew.

Chana's father worked for the United States Department of State in Washington DC, but for a few years he had been

---

* Not the real name.

stationed, together with his family, in Mexico City. That was just before Chana entered high school. As a result, she picked up Spanish, which she enjoyed speaking whenever she got the chance. Since she was attending the Ohel Sarah* Seminary in the Unsdorf neighborhood of Jerusalem, Chana got to know Rebbetzin Stein through the Shabbos hospitality program there.

Rabbi Dolinsky was delighted to hear about Chana. Not only did she speak Spanish, but she also exemplified the love and respect for Torah study that Asher was looking for in a wife. Rabbi Dolinsky was so excited with the *hashgachah pratis* of this suggested match that he could hardly wait to contact Asher's parents.

When he visited them, Benzion and Naomi Laniado were deeply touched that Rabbi Dolinsky was so concerned for their son that he had actually gone to speak with a matchmaker on his behalf.

Rabbi Dolinsky accepted the Laniados' gratitude and then quickly shifted the focus of the conversation to Chana. "She's an American girl who's in her second year at Ohel Sarah, here in Yerushalayim. I am told that she is a very special girl who is looking only for a *ben Torah*."

The Laniados were not very enthusiastic. Naomi Laniado spoke first. "To be quite honest, Rabbi, we really would prefer an Israeli girl for Asher. It's not just the language barrier. There are cultural differences, as well, which could interfere. I'm not sure that we would be interested."

"Of course," Rabbi Dolinsky agreed, "a common language is very important. But that's one of the reasons why, perhaps, you should consider this girl. She happens to speak fluent Spanish. Her name is Chana Shapiro. Maybe you'd like to ask around about her first?"

There was a long pause. Rabbi Dolinsky held his breath and then broke the silence. "Is there something wrong?" he asked, softly.

"No, not at all," Benzion replied. "But that name rings a

---

* Not the real name.

bell. I would like to check something and then get back to you."

Later that evening, Benzion called. "Is her father's name Larry, and does he work for the American government?" he asked tentatively.

Rabbi Dolinsky gasped. "Yes, his name *is* Larry," he replied. "And he works for the State Department. How do you know? Do you know the family?"

"Rabbi Dolinsky, you are not going to believe this. But I believe I met Chana's father. And not only that, but I think that *I* am responsible for her studying at Ohel Sarah!"

"You're right, I am having difficulty believing this," Rabbi Dolinsky whispered, feeling goosebumps all over. "Please tell me how you know Mr. Shapiro."

"Are you sure you have the time, now? It's a long story, Rabbi."

"Take all the time you need. And please, don't leave out any of the details."

Benzion took an audibly deep breath and began. "It must have been about three years ago that Larry Shapiro walked into my silver shop in Geula to buy a few gifts. Mr. Shapiro soon picked up my accent and asked if I spoke Spanish. When I told him that I grew up in Argentina, he quickly switched to Spanish, saying that he always looked for opportunities to brush up on his fluency.

"It was then that Mr. Shapiro explained to me that he worked for the United States Government and that was how he happened to learn Spanish. We really seemed to get rather chummy with each other quite quickly. I suppose the Spanish helped.

"Anyway, Mr. Shapiro went on to tell me that he was in Israel for only a few days. The main purpose of his trip was to find the right teachers' seminary for his daughter, who was then a high-school senior. He had visited a few of the local seminaries already. At that point, Mr. Shapiro had more or less made up his mind to send his daughter to the Teachers Training Seminary* in Yerushalayim.

---

* Not the real name.

"I certainly wasn't going to volunteer my opinion about TTS. But when he asked me if I had heard of it and what I thought about it, I felt free to offer my view.

"I told him that I thought he could do better for his daughter. Certainly TTS has a good academic record. But if he was sending his daughter to learn for a year, or possibly two, in Eretz Yisrael, I told him, he should also be concerned with how much inspiration she would receive. Did he want her to grow spiritually as well, or only intellectually?

"Mr. Shapiro was a bit taken aback by my assessment of TTS, but he really took in what I had to say. Then he asked if I could recommend another seminary which might provide what TTS was lacking.

"I told him about Ohel Sarah, and he liked what he heard. I then suggested that he not take my word for it but run over there to see for himself.

"He told me that he had only one more day left to his trip, but that if there were any way he could fit it in, he would certainly like to see Ohel Sarah for himself.

"I was quite amazed at how we seemed to hit it off so well in such a short amount of time. I guess the common language helped a lot. But whatever it was, we had established such rapport with each other that we exchanged addresses before he left my store. He said he wanted to be able to order items by mail in the future. And I said I wanted to find out where his daughter ended up.

"We did correspond a few times during that year. The last I heard, he had decided to apply to Ohel Sarah for his daughter and she had gotten accepted. I haven't heard from him since, but I saved his address nonetheless.

"That's why the name sounded familiar. But before I said anything, I wanted to check my card file to be sure it was the same Shapiro!"

Rabbi Dolinsky threw a couple of small branches on the fire and then sat down on the crate he was using for a chair. He let the meaning of his words sink in as the fire crackled.

Then he added the following epilogue.

"In case you're wondering how the *shidduch* worked out, I won't keep you in suspense. Asher and Chana met a few times and quickly became engaged. After they married, they moved to Bnei Brak, where they still live today. Asher is learning in *kollel*, and Chana works as an assistant principal in the same Bais Yaakov where she began teaching almost ten years ago.

"There is always *hashgachah pratis* involved whenever people find their *bashert* (preordained match). We know that every match is made in Heaven, but sometimes the guiding hand of *hashgachah* is especially obvious and revealed. The story of Asher and Chana is certainly a prime example of revealed *hashgachah*.

"Had I not gone to Rebbetzin Stein to ask for a *shidduch* for the first young man (who, by the way, also got married around the same time as Asher), I never would have heard about Chana.

"Had Larry Shapiro not been transferred to Mexico City, his daughter, Chana, would never have learned to speak Spanish. And if she did not speak Spanish, I never would have thought of Asher. It was also Chana's fluency in Spanish which made the Laniados even consider her, an American girl, as a match for their son.

"But of course the most amazing *hashgachah* of all is that Benzion Laniado tried so hard to convince a man who was an absolute stranger to send his daughter to a more spiritually oriented seminary. It is unusual that he even tried. And it is even more unusual that Larry Shapiro was willing to be influenced by this soft-spoken silver dealer.

"Had Chana attended the Teachers Training Seminary, she most likely would not have wanted to marry a man who was planning to learn in *kollel*. And after attending a seminary like TTS, she never would have been the type of girl Asher was looking for. But because Benzion Laniado succeeded in getting Chana's father to look into Ohel Sarah, he merited preparing her to become the type of wife his son ended up marrying.

"So one lesson we can learn from this story is how much a person can gain for himself by trying to help others. Benzion

Laniado wanted only to help a stranger and ended up planting the seeds of his own son's *shidduch*.

"Perhaps the most important lesson of this story, however, is that of *hashgachah pratis* itself. Just as we can see the Guiding Hand of Heaven in the lives of Asher and Chana, we must realize that the same Guiding Hand directs each of our lives... every day. It is the same Guiding Hand that has brought all of you here to learn in Eretz Yisrael... And it is the same Guiding Hand that has brought us together at this campfire tonight."

Rabbi Dolinsky lifted the straps of his accordion over his shoulders. Then he looked around the campfire and asked, "Who would like to start a *niggun*?"

[as heard from Rabbi Mordechai Dolinsky,
Kiryat Mattersdorf, Yerushalayim]

Measure for Measure

Mayer Isaacs* is a tall, low-keyed, somewhat reserved *kollel* student who lives in the Har Nof neighborhood of Yerushalayim. Originally from the midwest United States, he speaks with the gentle drawl of a man who is not in a hurry.

Mayer immigrated to Israel over ten years ago. At that time, his only plans were to learn in one of the city's renowned Yeshivos for a year or two. But then he met Sarah, who became his wife, and they decided to remain in Israel.

Mayer wears the traditional local garb of a long black coat and a wide-brimmed black hat which, together with his demeanor, helps him blend in with his surroundings. If you passed Mayer on the street, you would probably not notice him at all. But if you stopped to talk to him, you would find, beneath that unremarkable exterior, a breathtaking example of *middos tovos* — sterling character traits.

Mayer and Sarah are models of *emunah* and *bitachon* — faith and trust in Hashem. These two terms are often used interchangeably. To be more accurate, however, *emunah* refers to belief in the *hashgachah pratis* of Hashem, while *bitachon* refers to a life style which demonstrates *emunah*.

A good example of the Isaacs' *middos* is their commitment to *hachnasas orchim*. Even before they got married, Mayer and Sarah agreed that their home must always be open to guests. However much or little they would have, they felt, was a gift from Heaven which must be shared with others. So even though there were times when they did not know exactly how

---

* All the names in this story were changed by request.

51

they would make ends meet, they still made it a point never to refuse a guest.

As Mayer puts it, "I don't feel that I am giving something of mine away to others when we invite guests. On the contrary, I feel that whatever we have is being given to us only in the merit of the *mitzvos* we will perform with what we have. I suppose, in a way, we receive more from the merit of hosting our guests than they receive from us."

The Isaacs' appreciation of the benefits of *hachnasas orchim* really should have warranted their inclusion in my book, *AiSHeL: Contemporary Stories of Jewish Hospitality.** But, perhaps as a result of their unassuming natures, they were not "discovered" until recently. The following story illustrates not only how one may receive more than he gives, but also how that blessing takes the form of "measure for measure."

✧   ✧   ✧

Zev Eisner grew up in a typical, assimilated American Jewish home in a suburb of Los Angeles, California. Although he attended a Hebrew Day School until eighth grade, Zev did not continue his Jewish studies in high school. After a year in college, Zev felt disillusioned with himself, with life in general, and with his secular studies in particular.

On a summer trip to Israel, Zev attended the Discovery program, the three-day seminar sponsored by Yeshivah Aish Hatorah in Yerushalayim. Everything seemed to fall into place for Zev at the seminar and he decided to stay in Israel for a while and learn in a Yeshivah.

Zev was new to Orthodoxy, yet he was eager to learn. After a year of Yeshivah studies, he had made significant progress. But since he was such a shy young man, he had not succeeded in making many friends. While his fellow students always had loads of invitations for Shabbos meals, Zev found it difficult

_____

* Feldheim Publishers, 1994.

to cultivate relationships with prospective hosts. So, he often needed to be "set up" by the hospitality committee of the Yeshivah.

That was until Zev met the Isaacs family.

Zev first came to the Isaacs home on Pesach. From then on he knew he always had a place for Shabbos meals. It wasn't only because Mayer extended an open invitation, for Zev had received other such open invitations from other hosts; and it wasn't only because Zev felt that the Isaacs sincerely wanted guests, for Zev had been in other homes where guests were also permanent fixtures.

The reason Zev felt so comfortable in the Isaacs home was because his hosts were almost as shy as he was. Zev really felt relaxed in the home of this soft-spoken, gentle couple and their infant son. They never probed or challenged, never interrogated or prodded. If Zev did not feel like talking, that was fine for the Isaacs, who opened their hearts for Zev as wide as they opened their home.

In spite of how comfortable he felt in the Isaacs home, Zev nevertheless came for Shabbos only about once a month. The other weeks he either stayed in the dorm or ate with another family. He was always wary of imposing on the Isaacs and he hesitated calling more often for fear of wearing out his welcome.

In the five months after that first Pesach, although Zev had eaten with the Isaacs family only five times, he felt as if he had known them his whole life.

Three weeks before Sukkos, Zev was seated at the Isaacs' table on Saturday night, having spent an enjoyable Shabbos afternoon there. He turned to Mayer while Sarah was in the kitchen. "Uh, do you think I could be with you this year for Sukkos?"

"Of course," Mayer said immediately. "You know you're always welcome here. I'm glad you asked. I was meaning to invite you. We'd love to have you."

"Are you sure it's all right?" Zev asked. "Maybe you should check with your wife. After all, Sukkos is a whole week and I would need to sleep over since the Yeshivah will be closed during the holiday."

"If it will make you feel more comfortable, Zev, I'll discuss this with Sarah after you leave. Then I'll call you later this week to confirm. That way, you won't feel Sarah is being forced to agree because I'm asking her in front of you."

Zev smiled broadly and nodded. Somehow, Mayer always knew the right thing to say.

Later that evening, Mayer sat down with Sarah and told her of Zev's request.

"He wants to come for Sukkos?" Sarah could not contain her surprise. "Of course, I'd love to have him for the week. But where would he sleep?"

"He'll be sleeping with me in the *sukkah* all week," Mayer explained. "So I don't think he'll really be in the way."

"I'm not concerned about him 'being in the way'! You know I love having guests. But we have no extra bed," Sarah pointed out.

"That's true," Mayer acknowledged. "But I'm sure that between now and Sukkos, we'll be able to borrow at least a mattress for him. If he was asking us this much in advance, he must really want to be with us. How could we not agree?"

"You're right," Sarah said, and Mayer called Zev the same evening to confirm that he would be coming for the entire week of Sukkos.

As the Festival approached, Sarah found that the presumably simple task of borrowing a mattress proved more formidable than she and Mayer had anticipated. The neighbors across the hall were having company and could not spare any beds for Sukkos. Other friends across the street were planning to be away for Sukkos but they were renting out their apartment to a family who would need every bed... And so it was with everyone else Sarah asked.

Two days before Sukkos, Sarah began to get worried. She still had no bed or even a mattress for Zev. At supper that evening, Sarah mentioned her concern to Mayer.

"It's almost Sukkos and we haven't been able to find a bed

for Zev," Sarah noted uneasily. "What will we do?"

"I'm sure Hashem will help us," Mayer encouraged his wife. "We are only trying to do His will. Hashem has been so good to us in the past. I'm certain He will help us now, too."

"I just wish I had your *bitachon*, Mayer," Sarah confided. "But you know, a bed for Zev is not the only furniture we need now."

"Oh, Sarah, remember how Rabbi Akiva had only straw to sleep on and his wife complained they had no beds? Then a man came begging for straw on which to sleep. And that showed them how fortunate they were that they at least had straw. Well, we have real furniture and don't sleep on straw. How much more should we be thankful!"

"I am thankful, Mayer. But you know little Pinny is getting bigger and I can no longer feed him in his infant seat. What we really need now is a highchair."

"I wish we could afford to buy one, Sarah. But you know how impossible it is for us to buy something that expensive now. If we do not have the money to buy a highchair it means that we can probably manage for a little while longer without one. Hashem has always given us whatever we really needed in the past. Look, we were childless for almost nine years. Then Hashem answered our *tefillos* and Pinny was born. I know He will help us now, too."

Mayer tugged at his jet black beard. "You know, I just thought of someone else I could ask about a bed. I'll speak to him tonight."

The person Mayer had in mind turned out to be just as hospitable as Mayer and Sarah were — and therefore he had no extra beds for Sukkos!

The next day was *Erev Sukkos*. Even Mayer had begun to feel that his *emunah* was being tested. He still had no bed for Zev, who would be arriving in a few hours to spend the week with them. Maybe I could borrow a few cushions and put them together, Mayer thought to himself.

Not one to waste a minute, Mayer went out onto the porch

to complete building his *sukkah* . All the materials were there, but not yet assembled. Since it rarely rains in Israel during that time of the year, Mayer planned to spend his free day of *Erev Sukkos* erecting his *sukkah*.

Two hours into his construction work, Mayer was high atop a ladder with three nails in his mouth, a hammer in one hand and a heavy cross beam in the other. That's when the doorbell rang.

"Sarah, could you please answer the door," Mayer mumbled through a mouthful of nails.

Sarah was busy in the kitchen and could not hear Mayer above the loud humming of her electric mixer. So Mayer got down from his perch to see who was at the door.

It was Shia, another transplanted American *kollel* student, who lived down the block.

"I'm sorry to bother you on *Erev Sukkos*, Mayer, but I need a favor."

"Sure," Mayer shot back, without even hearing what the favor was. "For you, anything! Come on in."

Shia stepped inside and got right to the point. "You know we've been a bit crowded at home since the baby was born. And now my younger brother will be living with us for a few months until he can find a bed in the Yeshivah dormitory."

"Wow," Meyer observed. "You guys must be really tight for space. How can I help? Would you like me to take a couple of your kids for a while?"

Shia laughed. "No, but I'm sure you would do that if we asked! What I really need is a little storage space."

"Okay, Shia, tell me how I can help."

"Well..., uh, we have a couple of things we don't need right now but we'd rather not sell because we'll probably need them in the future. And if you have room to store them in your apartment for a while, it would give us a bit more room while my brother is with us. But if you can't, don't worry. I won't hold it against you."

"Look, Shia, if there's any way I can help you, I surely will. Tell me, what items do you need to store?"

"A folding bed...and if it's not asking too much, we also

have a highchair we won't be needing for a good few months."

✧　✧　✧

Mayer has told this story to many skeptics, so he knows how to emphasize the *hashgachah pratis*. "You might want to argue that Shia could have heard about our having Zev for Sukkos, and that we were looking to borrow a bed. Enough people in the neighborhood knew we were looking for one. Then you could claim that Shia made up the story of the 'favor' in order to offer the bed without embarrassing us.

"But there was absolutely no way that Shia could have known that the night before, Sarah and I were talking about needing a highchair!

"Clearly our needs were known by the One Who takes care of all our needs."

[Hashem] opens up His hand and satisfies every living being according to his needs.

TEHILLIM 145:16

[as heard from Mayer Isaacs,
Har Nof, Jerusalem]

A Gulf War Nugget

Thursday, January 17, 1991, was a day that will be forever remembered as the start of the Gulf War. Although the State of Israel never officially entered the war, it most reluctantly occupied center stage throughout that conflict. Not only were the eyes of world Jewry riveted on Israel, but pivotal events themselves also revolved around this tiny Jewish country.

During the course of the war, a total of 39 deadly SCUD missiles were fired from Iraq and aimed at major population centers in Israel. Some of the missiles were intercepted in midair by American Patriot missiles, providing a surrealistic fireworks display in the midnight sky over Tel Aviv. The majority of the missiles exploded on the ground; but, miraculously, only one person was killed from all of the missile attacks.

Throughout the war, the protective Hand of Heaven was acknowledged by both secular as well as religious Jews. The accounts of *hashgachah pratis* were so numerous that people almost took them for granted. It even felt like a matter of course for lives to be saved in most unusual ways during the Gulf War.

After entire apartment buildings were crushed by the impact of missile blasts, it seemed impossible for anyone to have survived. Nevertheless, time and again, the rubble was cleared and no casualties were discovered. How could this be? Everyone wondered. Then slowly the evidence emerged.

One person was supposed to be here, but for some reason was there. A door that should have been open was locked, while a door that should have been locked was open. Over and over again, people found themselves where they did not want to be or where they never suspected they would go, only to discover that their last-minute change of plans saved their lives.

If you wanted to write a book on *hashgachah pratis* , you would have more than enough material by simply collecting all of the golden accounts of miraculous, supernatural events which saved countless lives during the Gulf War. What follows is but one small nugget from that rich mine of inspiration which took place in our own lifetime.

If you are the aggressor, you want to attack when your victims will be least able to defend themselves. For that reason, Saddam Hussein chose the late night hours to fire his deadly missiles toward Israel.

At night, the country would be less prepared and alert. At night most people would be in their homes. And the night is when people usually try to sleep, which was rendered impossible by the constant threat of yet another missile attack.

During the day, people in Israel were more or less assured that the SCUDs would not be coming. But towards nightfall, fear mounted as everyone wondered if tonight's half-sleep would be shattered again by the wail of sirens.

While all of Israel held their breath each night, the residents of the Tel Aviv area suffered the most. As the largest population center in the country, the area was Hussein's prime target. Most of the SCUDs were aimed at that residential jugular vein of the country in attempts to inflict the greatest number of casualties.

When the sirens did go off, the residents of Israel were instructed by civil service radio broadcasts to enter their "sealed rooms," put on their gas masks, and await further instructions.

A sealed room was a room at home that had been prepared by every family in advance, as protection from a chemical attack. All of the windows were sealed with plastic. Bottles of boiled water and nonperishable foods were kept there in the event that the family might have to remain there for any great length of time. Towels were also prepared which were to be soaked in water and placed over the threshold of the door to further seal the room once everyone was inside.

Sitting in a sealed room was a nerve-wracking experience, at best. With the bulky gas masks in place, conversation was impossible. Family members could only communicate in sign language. Hearts pounded as people recited *Tehillim*, listened to the radio, or simply held hands for moral support. It wasn't a time that anyone wanted to be alone.

✧   ✧   ✧

One night at 2:00 AM, the siren as usual jolted those who were sleeping, out of their beds. Everyone instinctively rushed into their sealed rooms, in what had become a familiar routine, especially in Tel Aviv, where most of the SCUDs had fallen. Everyone, that is, except Meir and Zvi Malkhan, two single brothers living on their own.

They were on their way into their sealed room when Meir stopped his brother. "Zvi, I'm worried about Mrs. Yona. She's all alone in her apartment. And because of the recent attacks, all her neighbors in the building have moved out temporarily. She must be terrified now."

"You're right, Meir. Let's go over and ask her to join us in our sealed room until the all-clear is sounded. I'm sure she'll feel better being with us than all by herself."

The two Malkhan brothers grabbed their gas masks and headed out into the hall and down the stairs. Once on the street, they looked up and saw the lights on in other apartment buildings as people were busy hurrying into their sealed rooms. But in their building, only the lights in their apartment were on, for their neighbors too had made other arrangements. Because of the enormous danger involved, as well as the lateness of the hour, the street itself was totally deserted.

Meir and Zvi dashed into the building next door and bounded up the steps to the fourth-floor apartment of Naima

Yona, an elderly widow who was a friend of the Malkhan family. They rang the doorbell and waited, panting breathlessly.

Naima answered the door. "Zvi and Meir? What on earth are you boys doing here, now? Didn't you hear the siren? You should go home immediately and get inside your sealed room. The middle of a missile attack is no time to be outside!"

"Mrs. Yona," Meir gasped, still trying to catch his breath, "we *were* at home. That's where we're coming from now. But we came over here to take you to our apartment. We figured you would feel more secure waiting out the attack with us."

"Oh, you boys are so kind, but it is really not necessary. True, all of my neighbors in the building made arrangements to sleep in Yerushalayim, since they thought they'd be safer there. But you should know that I have my own sealed room here — you yourselves were thoughtful enough to tape up my windows."

"Mrs. Yona," Zvi pleaded, "we really need to get back home, now. But we are simply not going without you. You'll still have other opportunities to use your own sealed room, I'm afraid. But for tonight, please come with us. You'll feel better at this hour waiting with other people."

Naima chuckled softly. "You boys are very convincing... all right, I'll be right with you. Just let me just go in and get my gas mask and my house keys. Don't worry, I won't keep you waiting."

Naima Yona quickly locked up her apartment and made her way down the four flights of steps as quickly as she could with Meir and Zvi Malkhan supporting her on either side.

As the threesome were about midway between the two adjacent buildings they heard a sudden whizzing sound. They froze in their places and watched in horror as a SCUD missile landed in the alley between their two buildings. The missile exploded immediately with ear-splitting intensity. All three of them covered their ears in a vain attempt to block out some of the piercing sound.

With the explosion, both Naima's building and that of the Malkhan brothers were completely destroyed. The walls closest to the blast collapsed first, and then both buildings folded in like houses of cards. The dust rose together with the rising smoke.

Meir, Zvi, and Naima stood motionless on the sidewalk, trying to absorb what had just taken place. In a few seconds, both of their homes had been completely destroyed. Miraculously, not only was no one killed, but there were not even any injuries.

All of the neighbors in their buildings were miles away in the relative safety of Yerushalayim, where no SCUDs had fallen, and this threesome realized immediately that their lives were saved by the remarkable timing of *hashgachah pratis*.

All three realized that had it not been for the concern of the Malkhan brothers, none of them would still be standing alive at that moment. Clearly, their act of *chesed* saved them all. But had they not been standing *in between* both buildings at the *precise* moment when the missile landed, they would not have lived to tell the story. A few seconds longer before Meir and Zvi had left their own building or a few seconds less when they had stood talking with Naima — and they would not have been in the right spot at the exactly the right time.

When Meir, Zvi, and Naima looked around, they found themselves surrounded by head-shaking, wide-eyed neighbors from nearby buildings who had rushed outside after the blast to assist any possible victims. The throng of Tel Avivians buzzed with wonderment when they discovered that there were no casualties... and then learned why.

[as heard from Rabbi Dovid Finkelman, Brooklyn, New York
and corroborated in Yediot Acharonot, Jan. 20, 1991
and Yated Ne'eman, Feb. 15, 1991]

Shopping for Vegetables

One of the most beloved and favorite *zemiros* (liturgical songs) sung in many homes on Friday night is *Ka Ribbon Olam*. This song of praise to Hashem concludes with the words, "*bi-Yerushalem karta d'shufraya.*"

This phrase is often translated as, "in Yerushalayim the beautiful city." Some commentators, however, have noted that a more correct translation of the Aramaic words *karta d'shufraya* would be "city of the beautiful ones," a reference to the many beautiful, holy, and righteous souls who live in that eternal city.

✧   ✧   ✧

One of the beautiful souls who inhabited the Mea Shearim neighborhood of Yerushalayim until his recent passing was Reb Elya Roth, *zatzal*. Reb Elya was a beacon of light and source of inspiration to anyone who had the unique good fortune to have met him.

In addition to his exemplary piety and steadfast devotion to serving Hashem, Reb Elya was best known for his most contagious joy and his utter trust in Hashem.

A young *kollel* student was once mildly depressed over a sudden financial setback. His *Rosh Yeshivah* suggested that he go to Reb Elya for encouragement.

"Who is Reb Elya and how can he encourage me?" the young man wanted to know. His *Rosh Yeshivah* simply gave him Reb Elya's address and told the young man to return after the visit if he still had questions.

The young man came to Reb Elya's tiny, delapidated apartment. From the open doorway he saw Reb Elya sitting at a cluttered table learning from a tattered *sefer*. An adult retarded son was sitting off to the side of the same room, uttering undecipherable sounds to himself. Reb Elya's wife, who was known to be mentally ill, was shouting curses at him from another room.

The young man cautiously approached Reb Elya and gingerly sat down on the edge of the only empty chair in the room. Before he could explain the purpose of his visit, Reb Elya turned to him, and his glowing face, surrounded by the halo of his white beard and *peyos*, broke into a huge smile.

"Do you realize how fortunate I am?" Reb Elya asked his startled visitor. "From where I am sitting right now, I am able to look out and see the gorgeous blue midday sky of Yerushalayim. I don't even have to get up out of my chair. How could I ever thank Hashem enough for all of his blessings?"

Reb Elya continued in that vein for another minute or two. The young man then got up, thanked Reb Elya, and left. He didn't need to explain the purpose of his visit. He had found what he was looking for, and he understood why his *Rosh Yeshivah* had sent him.

✧   ✧   ✧

In his later years, Reb Elya was so frail and infirm that he was able to visit the Kosel only twice a year. He made it a practice to go only on *chol ha-mo'ed* (the intermediate days) of Pesach and Sukkos. As he would explain, the Kosel is the place where the Divine Presence rests. And the Rabbis have taught that the *Shechinah* rests only on someone who is in a state of joy (see *Shabbos* 30b). And so, since Reb Elya felt that he achieved sufficient joy only on the Festivals, it was only then that he would permit himself to pray at the Kosel.

He considered the trip itself to the Kosel so holy that he would not want to share the merit with a vehicle of any kind.

Therefore, he walked all the way there and all the way back. Because he was so old, the entire round trip typically took him all day. Along the way he was often accompanied by those experienced Yerushalayim residents who knew that this was often a rare opportunity to hear Reb Elya speak his words of insight and inspiration.

Reb Elya was someone who did not "believe in" *hashgachah pratis* — he lived it and breathed it, every moment of his life. For Reb Elya Roth, *hashgachah pratis* was not a concept or outlook. It was rather the essence of his very soul that was inextricably woven into the fiber of his being. The following brief anecdote is but a footnote to the intimate awareness of *hashgachah pratis* which filled his life.

✧ ✧ ✧

Reb Elya needed some vegetables. This sounds simple enough — but what for us would be a routine chore was for Reb Elya an opportunity for greatness.

Reb Elya's wife, due to her unfortunate condition, was not able to assist in managing the Roth home. Therefore, when they needed vegetables, Reb Elya knew that he would have to go to the market himself to get them.

With his octogenarian shuffle, Reb Elya made his way out of his home and down the street to the *shuk*, the open-air market. When he reached the first vegatable stand, he began to take a few tomatoes and place them into a plastic bag.

Just then, Rabbi Nochum Cohen, the *menahel* of the Sadigerre Yeshivah in Yerushalayim, came walking by. Rabbi Cohen recognized a golden opportunity to catch a few words of inspiration from this spiritual giant.

Ducking under the makeshift awning of the vegetable stand to block the rays of the late-morning sun, Rabbi Cohen respectfully greeted the venerable sage. "*Shalom aleichem*, Reb Elya! How are you today?"

Reb Elya responded with a gentle nod and a common phrase which had much deeper meaning coming from him:

"*Baruch Hashem!*"

Rabbi Cohen noticed that Reb Elya seemed to be paying almost no attention to the tomatoes he was gathering from the large pile in front of him. "Reb Elya, why do you take from the top of the pile? Why not take from underneath where the better ones are?"

Reb Elya stopped what he was doing to look up at his younger friend, who stood a full foot taller. In the matter-of-fact tone one uses to explain the obvious, Reb Elya taught Rabbi Cohen a valuable lesson in *bitachon*: "If these tomatoes are on top of the pile and easier for me to get to, then it means that they are the ones that are meant for me to take."

Reb Elya turned back to his task and continued to slowly fill his plastic bag with vegetables.

"And how are you managing at home?" Rabbi Cohen asked Reb Elya. "Is there anything that I could get or do for you?"

Genuinely surprised, Reb Elya responded, "Why do you ask me such questions? Am I a single man who lives alone? I have a wife at home to care for me."

"But, Reb Elya," Rabbi Cohen proceeded cautiously, "perhaps your wife is not feeling well today and is not able to do some of her usual chores?"

"Because she is not well today, does not mean that she won't be well tomorrow," Reb Elya shot back, almost annoyed that Rabbi Cohen had not realized this on his own.

The two men continued chatting as Reb Elya handed his purchase to the vendor, who quickly weighed the vegetables. A religious man himself, the vendor did not want to interrupt Reb Elya's conversation to announce the price.

A few moments passed and the vendor became impatient. Finally, he spoke up. "That will be five shekels, please."

Reb Elya did not acknowledge the vendor and continued expounding upon a verse in that week's Torah portion. The vendor repeated the price, this time a little louder, but to no avail. Reb Elya was completely engrossed by now in his conversation with Rabbi Cohen. Neither the vendor nor Rabbi Cohen felt comfortable enough to grab Reb Elya's attention more forcefully.

A few moments later, Rabbi Cohen broke the mini-stalemate by reaching into his own pocket for the money and handing it to the vendor. Reb Elya picked up his vegetables and turned toward home, still accompanied by Rabbi Cohen.

Rabbi Cohen offered to carry the vegetables for Reb Elya. In his characteristic fashion, Reb Elya politely refused, saying he was, thank God, well and strong enough to carry them himself.

After the two had walked on another few yards, Rabbi Cohen broke the silence. "Reb Elya, didn't you notice that the vendor was waiting to be paid just now? Why did you ignore him and continue talking with me?"

Reb Elya answered in the same matter-of-fact tone as before. "I didn't pay him because I had no money."

"Then why didn't you just say you had no money with you and you would return later with money from home?" Rabbi Cohen asked, trying to conceal his amazement.

"I couldn't say that to the vendor because I have no money at home, either," replied Reb Elya, as he shuffled along the narrow sidewalk.

"But Reb Elya," Rabbi Cohen persisted, his voice rising a little, "how can you possibly go shopping for vegetables when you know you have no money? What did you think when you left your house? How did you expect to pay?"

Reb Elya stopped now and looked up at Rabbi Cohen. "As I've told you many times, Reb Nochum, Hashem takes care of everyone. Hashem provides whatever we need, whenever we need it."

"But Reb Elya, if you left the house without any money, how did you expect Hashem to pay for your vegetables?"

Reb Elya looked at Rabbi Cohen and shook his head, as if to say, "I don't see why this is difficult for you to understand." Leaning on his cane, he took a deep breath. "Look, Reb Nochum, could I have known before I left my house that Hashem would send *you* to stop and pay for my vegetables?... I knew that Hashem would take care of me — I did not need to know how."

Rabbi Nochum Cohen especially relishes retelling this particular encounter with Reb Elya.

"Of course, we all believe that Hashem takes care of us," Rabbi Cohen observes. "That is one of the fundamentals of our *emunah*. But how many of us could actually go shopping for vegetables without a penny in our pocket and not be the least concerned with how we will pay for them? The only person I know who was capable of that was Reb Elya, *zatzal*."

Then Rabbi Cohen adds with a chuckle, "But then again, how many of us would be worthy of having someone come along, just when we needed him, to pay for our vegetables? I suppose Reb Elya taught us all how Heaven repays our trust with *hashgachah pratis*. And that is a lesson that no one could teach better than Reb Elya, *zatzal*. May his merit protect us all."

[as heard from Rabbi Nochum Cohen,
Geula, Yerushalayim]

Change for Tzedakah

The late afternoon sun cast long shadows across Rechov Sorotzkin in the Unsdorf neighborhood of Yerushalayim. With less than an hour before Shabbos, the normally bustling street was now quiet, reflecting the serenity of *Erev Shabbos* in the neighborhood. A few younger children, already dressed in their Shabbos clothes, played peacefully on the sidewalk.

Running down the stairs of the apartment building where my family and I had rented an apartment, I burst out onto the street in search of a taxi. My son, Yeshaya, who was ten years old at the time, quickly caught up with me. "Ta," he asked me breathlessly, "are you sure you have enough money this time? Remember what happened last week!"

This was our third Shabbos of a four-week vacation in Eretz Yisrael. The week before, my family had also taken a taxi to the Kosel on Friday afternoon, and then had walked back to eat with relatives after *davening*. This week, my wife had decided to forgo praying at the Kosel in order to have more time to visit with some other relatives. So, since my fourteen-year-old daughter, Sarah, was at camp in the States, just Yeshaya and I were out searching for a taxi.

Yeshaya clearly wanted to avoid a repeat performance of the nerve-wracking haggling that had gone on the week before. Then, the three of us had anxiously approached every taxi that I hailed, and each time the driver quoted a price that was slightly higher than the amount of money I had brought with me. Not wanting to be left with too much spare change at the Kosel right before Shabbos entered, I thought I had estimated exactly how much the fare would be. Maybe I *under*estimated, since we had to go through four taxis and quite a bit of bargaining before we found a driver willing to make the trip for the amount of money I had with me.

This week I was prepared. "Yes, Yeshaya, I took extra money this time. Since most of the drivers last week were asking for ten shekels, I took thirteen just to be on the safe side," I called over my shoulder to the sidewalk as I stood in the street looking in both directions.

"Maybe you should have taken a little *more*, to be sure?" Yeshaya asked nervously.

"Are you kidding?" I turned all the way around this time. "There's no way it could be more than ten, maybe twelve shekels. You'll see."

As bus service had already stopped, only taxis and a few private cars whizzed by as we stood on the street. We weren't the only ones looking for a cab so most of the taxis were already full. Pretty soon, however, one did pull up.

"How much to the Kosel?" I asked in Hebrew.

The driver hesitated, sized me up and then replied in English, "Thirteen shekels."

Yeshaya and I jumped in. I shot a knowing, "I told you so," glance to Yeshaya as he shot back a look of, "Whew! I'm glad that's over."

I'm not surprised he could tell I am an American, I mused. My accent must have given me away. But how did he know that I had exactly thirteen shekels in my pocket!

"Ta, what would you have done with the extra three shekels if the price was only ten, like you thought?" Yeshaya wanted to know as the taxi barreled down Rechov Sorotzkin.

"I was planning to give them to *tzedakah*," I shouted, trying to be heard above the crackling of the driver's two-way radio.

"How could you do that?" Yeshaya persisted. "Do poor people collect *tzedakah* at the Kosel so close before Shabbos?"

"No, of course not," I explained. "There's a *pushke* at the Kosel where people can contribute money towards the upkeep of the plaza and for the purchase of *siddurim*."

Now, I thought to myself, Hashem had other plans for those three shekels and they won't be going for *tzedakah*, after all.

The driver broke in on my thoughts. "I'm terribly sorry about this, but I'm going to have to let you off when we get to Rechov Bar Ilan. Don't worry about getting to the Kotel, though, because you'll have no trouble at all getting a taxi from there. They pass by all the time."

"Why can't you take us all the way?" I asked. "There's still at least half an hour before candle-lighting time."

The driver gave an embarrassed laugh. "No, that's not why I can't take you. My dispatcher took a phone reservation from Ramot and he insists that I go there now. I explained to him that I just picked up a fare on the street but he won't listen to me."

"That's okay, I understand," I relented as the taxi came to a stop. "How much do I owe you for the ride this far?"

"You know," the driver said, sheepishly, "what I'm doing now is really illegal. I could lose my taxi license for not taking you all the way to your destination after picking you up. So, since you are being so understanding about this... you don't owe me anything. *Shabbat Shalom*."

Yeshaya and I waited for the light and then crossed the busy street. By the time we got to the other side I had already flagged down another taxi. "How much to the Kosel?" I asked in Hebrew.

"Ten shekels," he replied in English.

Yeshaya and I jumped in. He may be able to tell that I'm an American, I thought, but he can't tell how much money I have in my pocket — so I suppose I'll have those three shekels change left for the *pushke*, after all.

I leaned back to enjoy the ride through the already empty streets of Mea Shearim. The children's freshly scrubbed faces shone with anticipation of the holy Shabbos. Some men, wearing the traditional *Yerushalmi* gold-striped robes, with fur *shtreimlach* on their heads, were already walking leisurely to shul. Their relaxed pace was contrasted sharply with the speed of the taxi. It wasn't that close to Shabbos, but perhaps the driver was still hoping to pick up another fare or two before going home.

Along the way, I reflected on the strange turn of events which would now enable to me to fulfill my original plan to contribute three shekels to *tzedakah* at the Kosel.

As we a drove through the Old City approaching the entrance to the Kosel plaza, our taxi joined what looked like a convoy of taxis. Of almost a dozen cars that pulled up to the curb together, only two were private cars. Clearly, we were not the only ones taking taxis to the Kosel for Friday night services.

Yeshaya and I blended with the crowd getting in line to enter the security gate. Someone behind me was shouting, obviously not for me, so I did not bother to turn around. The shouts came closer and then I felt a tap on the shoulder. When I turned around I was faced with a visibly distraught *Yeshivah bocher* about 15 or 16 years old whom I did not recognize.

"Hi, how are you? You know me, don't you? I learn in Yeshivas Novominsk, where you *daven*." The words tumbled out of his mouth in anxious spurts.

Being the jaded, street-smart New York that I am, I immediately discounted the accurate tidbit of information this young man had picked up. Sure, I thought, I do *daven* at the Novominsk *Beis Midrash*, but his knowing that fact hardly compensates for the unfamiliar face of this agitated fellow.

"No," I shook my head. "I don't think I know you."

"Tatty," Yeshaya tried to grab my attention as he tugged at my arm. "He does learn in Novominsk. I've seen him in shul a few times."

My guard began to drop. With a spark of hope in his eyes, the young man continued breathlessly, "Maybe you could help us? We're in some trouble right now — you see, me and four other guys took a taxi to the Kosel but we're a little short for the fare. Turns out the driver is an Arab, and he's real mad at us — says he won't let us out of his cab until he gets all of his money. When I saw you just now I said, 'Hey, I know that guy. Maybe he'll lend us the extra money!' Listen, if you could lend us the money, I promise I'll come on *motza'ei Shabbos* to wherever you're staying and pay you back. I'm really sorry to put you on the spot like this, but as you can see we're desperate."

I did believe his story, but I did not see how I could help. "I'm already Shabbosdik," I said apologetically. "I don't have my wallet with me."

His face fell, but by this point, I really wanted to help him. As an afterthought I asked, "How much money do you still owe the driver?"

"Three shekels."

Three shekels?! All he needed was three shekels! I felt numb as I reached into my pocket and took out the three shekels.

The young man's face lit up like a sky rocket. "Oh, thank you! Please, please tell me where you're staying so I can repay you after Shabbos."

"That really isn't necessary," I said, still overwhelmed by the fact that the amount this boy so desperately needed was *exactly* the amount of change I had in my pocket. "But if you insist on repaying me, give three shekels to *tzedakah* for me after Shabbos."

"Oh sure, sure! Thank you so much, and *Gut Shabbos.*" The young man ran off to liberate his comrades as Yeshaya and I proceeded to the Kosel.

"Ta, you really did the right thing by giving him the money, but I guess now you won't be able to give the three shekels to *tzedakah* like you wanted," Yeshaya commented with a note of disappointment.

I stopped in my tracks, oblivious to the swirls of people gathering at the Kosel square and passing us by from all directions. "Yeshaya, don't you realize that I did give *tzedakah* just now? I didn't put the money in the *pushke* at the Kosel as I had planned, but I most certainly did use the money for *tzedakah*. In fact, I may have been able to fulfill another mitzvah at the same time."

"Really?" Yeshaya's eyes widened. "Which mitzvah?"

"*Pidyon shevuyim* — redeeming Jewish captives." I elaborated: "Those boys were really afraid to leave the taxi. They may have even felt that they were being held captive. By giving them the three shekels, we were responsible for their being 'freed.' Tomorrow night the boys will put three shekels in a *pushke* somewhere, which will be fulfilling the mitzvah of *tzedakah* for us. But now, we may have also fulfilled the very critical mitzvah of *pidyon shevuyim*, about which the *Shulchan Aruch* says there is no greater mitzvah." (See *Yoreh De'ah*, Vol. III, Chap. 252, para. 1.)

"Wow!" Yeshaya's chest heaved with pride. "So I guess it was lucky for us that the first taxi driver couldn't take us, right?"

"No, Yeshaya." I replied, smiling. "It wasn't luck. It was *hashgachah pratis*."

Then we walked on to the Kosel and I planted a long kiss on the ancient stones in appreciation for the special Providence which we had just experienced.

On the Bus

It was the night of Purim. The *Megillah* had just been read at Yeshivah Ohavei Torah* and now the boys, eager to break the fast of *Ta'anis Esther*, were spilling out onto the streets of Bnei Brak, energized by the anticipation of the lively celebrations that were to come later that night and the next day.

After the first wave exited the Yeshivah, Rabbi Matisyahu Danziger slowly walked out and headed to the bus stop. Rabbi Danziger, a healthy man in his late 50's, left the Yeshivah slowly for two reasons. First, he always walked out slowly as sign of respect for the sanctity of the Yeshivah. Second, as the beloved *mashgiach* that he was, he was always surrounded by a swarm of boys whenever he entered or left the Yeshivah. They would either try to engage him in conversation or at least listen in on a conversation he was having with someone else. As a result, he found it especially difficult to enter or leave the Yeshivah quickly.

Since Rabbi Danziger was so slow in leaving the Yeshivah that night he missed his bus and had to wait for another one. This did not upset him in the least. "It was obviously not meant for me to ride that bus tonight," he explained to his devoted students as they waited with him at the bus stop.

Ten minutes later, Rabbi Danziger's bus arrived and he moved aside to allow the crowd of exiting passengers to step onto the sidewalk. The last two passengers off the bus were a young couple who did not notice anyone except each other — but the Rabbi noticed the young man.

---

* All of the names in this story were changed by request.

"Rafi!" Rabbi Danziger called out. "How are you? How have you been?"

"Oh, Rabbi Danziger," Rafi replied, somewhat startled by the unexpected meeting. "A *freiliche* Purim. I am, *Baruch Hashem*, very well, very well indeed. Let me introduce you to my *kallah*. This is Baila. We were married last month."

"*Mazal Tov* to you both. May you merit to build a *bayis ne'eman b'Yisrael*. I am so happy to hear such good news," Rabbi Danziger exclaimed, as his bus pulled away from the curb without him.

Rafi looked a bit embarrassed by the flood of good wishes. "I suppose I really should have invited you, Rebbe, but we actually had a very short engagement and didn't have a big wedding and..."

"Rafi, I understand. After all, it has been quite a few years since you left the Yeshivah, and we lost touch with each other. You can't invite the whole world. But please, tell me how you met."

"Rebbe, *how* we met would not interest you. But *why* we met — I know that would interest you."

Rabbi Danziger sensed that Rafi might be embarrassed to tell his story in front of all of the boys who were waiting at the bus stop with him. So he asked Rafi to call him later that evening at home, which Rafi agreed to do.

It had been four years since Rabbi Danziger had even spoken with Rafi. But because of the events which had transpired between the two, Rabbi Danziger had never forgotten him.

When Rabbi Danziger finally did board his bus, he settled down on a seat and let his mind wander back to the stressful episode which had precipitated Rafi's leaving Yeshivah Ohavei Torah.

✧ ✧ ✧

Rafi came to the Yeshivah straight out of high school in America. He had never been to Israel before and was very unaccustomed to the way of life there. Adjustment to Israeli food, dormitory life, and Israeli culture in general, was difficult for Rafi. He did not make friends easily and had a hard time keeping study partners. In short, he was a student who took up an inordinate amount of Rabbi Danziger's time.

With many hours of gentle encouragement, soft words, and plenty of guidance, Rafi did eventually settle in to Yeshivah life. After three years in Ohavei Torah, his character improvement was noticeable to all.

But, as a leopard never changes its spots, some character traits are harder to change than others. And one aspect of Rafi's personality remained uncorrected, in spite of Rabbi Danziger's best efforts. Rafi had a stubborn streak and could not give in, if he felt he was right about something. His friends and study partners learned to accommodate to this character flaw, but there finally came an incident in which Rafi's stubbornness upset the tranquillity of the entire Yeshivah.

Rafi had come into the Yeshivah office looking for Rabbi Danziger. As he stood in the outer office he heard two Rebbeim talking in one of the inner offices. None of the secretaries were at their desks, so Rafi did not hesitate to eavesdrop on the conversation to determine if one of the voices was that of Rabbi Danziger.

Before he was able to identify the two voices, Rafi had heard enough of the conversation to pique his curiosity. Then it was too late to walk away. He was glued to his place just outside the doorway.

What he overheard was a conversation between Rabbi Tuvia Stein, one of the administrators, and Rabbi Anshel Gross, one of the teachers. Rabbi Stein was trying to convince Rabbi Gross to accept Rabbi Stein's nephew into his class, even though Rabbi Gross did not feel the nephew deserved to be included in this more advanced and prestigious *shiur.*

Rafi was outraged that a member of the administration of the Yeshivah would try to use his position to influence one of the Rebbeim regarding a class placement. In righteous indignation, Rafi turned around and marched straight to the *Rosh Yeshivah*'s study to report his discovery.

Rabbi Stein was a well-liked and well-respected member of the Ohavei Torah staff. The *Rosh Yeshivah* did not defend Rabbi Stein's behavior, but, nonetheless, he did defend Rabbi Stein's reputation. He then suggested that Rafi talk this all over with Rabbi Danziger.

Rabbi Danziger tried to calm Rafi down and agreed to investigate the incident. In the meantime, he begged Rafi not to repeat what he heard to any other students.

Rafi listened to Rabbi Danziger and tried to contain himself for a few days. But when he saw that "nothing was being done" about the matter, he did "spread the word" about what Rabbi Stein "was really like" to the other boys in the Yeshivah.

When confronted by Rabbi Danziger for having spoken *lashon ha-ra*, Rafi justified and rationalized his actions. Rabbi Stein was, of course, deeply embarrassed by all of this. Even though the Yeshivah's staff tried to convince him to stay, he felt too ashamed to remain at the Yeshivah. Two weeks after the episode was publicized by Rafi, Rabbi Stein announced his resignation.

Rabbi Danziger came to Rafi numerous times during those two weeks and practically begged Rafi to apologize to Rabbi Stein. "It's true that he shouldn't have tried to use his pull for his nephew," Rabbi Danziger explained, "but nothing can excuse the suffering and great shame you have caused him. At least now, before he leaves, ask him to forgive you."

"But Rebbe, why should I apologize?" Rafi replied. "Any embarrassment he has suffered is his own fault. He should have thought twice before he acted. It was an accident that I overheard the conversation. But if I had it to do over again, I would do the same thing!"

Rafi stayed on at Ohavei Torah for two more years after Rabbi Stein left. Then, at the age of 23, he also decided to leave. Most of Rafi's friends had either returned to America or had gotten married. In spite of his going out on numerous dates, Rafi had not succeeded in finding the right girl.

Rafi felt out of place among the younger boys. He also felt slightly embarrassed that he was not yet married. He knew that he needed to move on, so he accepted a position as a teacher at a Yeshivah which was somewhat more modern than Ohavei Torah.

During the first year after leaving Ohavei Torah, Rafi maintained his ties with Rabbi Danziger, visiting with him about once every two months. Mostly, they talked about Rafi's unsuccessful attempts at finding a *shidduch*.

It was during this time that Rafi developed some stubborn gastrointestinal problems. Regardless of which doctor Rafi consulted, his medical problems were not relieved. Since Rafi's own father was a top cardiologist in America, he had the resources to find and pay for the best medical attention Israel had to offer. Nevertheless, Rafi's condition not only did not improve but it also seemed to deteriorate.

Rabbi Danziger gently encouraged Rafi once more to apologize to Rabbi Stein.

"I'm sorry, Rebbe. I just cannot do that. I did nothing wrong and there is no reason for me to apologize. I see what you're getting at, but I don't see why that should have anything to do with my difficulties."

After that conversation, Rabbi Danziger lost contact with Rafi.

Rabbi Danziger had been home from Ohavei Torah almost an hour and was beginning to wonder whether or not Rafi would call as he had promised. Just then the phone rang.

"Hello, Rabbi Danziger, it's Rafi. Have you had a chance to finish eating after the fast?"

"Yes, of course. It's so nice to hear from you, Rafi. Thank you for calling. I'm eager to hear 'why' you met your *kallah*, as you put it."

"Well, Rebbe," Rafi began, "do you remember that whole episode I had with Rabbi Stein?"

"Uh, yes, Rafi, I certainly do."

"Well, six months ago I was riding the bus home from the Yeshivah where I teach. After a few stops, I looked up from the *sefer* I was studying and noticed that the route looked unfamiliar. I asked another passenger which bus I was on and was reassured that I had gotten on the right bus. Then I suddenly realized that it was, indeed, the right number but I was going in the wrong direction! I must have absentmindedly taken the bus going in the opposite direction.

"As soon as I realized what I'd done, I got up and made my way toward the door to get off at the next stop. The bus was quite crowded, so I could not get through the aisle easily.

"Just before I reached the door, I came face-to-face with Rabbi Stein. I hadn't seen him since he left Ohavei Torah. And I didn't even know where he lived. But since I never took the bus in the opposite direction, I suppose that's why I'd never met him on that bus before.

"I was about to get off and just ignore him, but I suddenly remembered how hard you'd tried to get me to apologize to him, and how you said that maybe I was having stomach problems and such a hard time with *shidduchim* because of the suffering I had caused him. So I took a deep breath and asked him for *mechilah*.

"I told him that I was sorry I had embarrassed him publicly and that he'd ended up leaving the Yeshivah because of what I had done.

"He was really very gracious about the whole thing. He smiled, shook my hand and told me he forgave me with a full heart. When I got off the bus, I knew I had done the right thing.

"A week later, I met Baila. So I guess you were right, Rebbe, about why I was not getting married. After having dated unsuccessfully for over seven years, I met my *kallah* just a few days after asking Rabbi Stein for forgiveness. So I really have to thank you for pushing me like you did."

"Rafi," Rabbi Danziger told him joyfully, "I'm so happy to hear that you asked Rabbi Stein to forgive you. But you must explain something to me. After all these years, what do you think enabled you to ask for *mechilah* now?"

"Well, Rebbe, you know how difficult it was for me. And I don't think I would have actually initiated it on my own. But when I came face-to-face with Rabbi Stein on the bus, I realized that it was no coincidence. I just couldn't escape the *hashgachah pratis* of our meeting. I felt as if I were being taken by the hand and led, like a stubborn little boy, to do what I should have done a long time ago."

Rabbi Danziger sighed deeply and audibly. There was a brief silence and then he asked Rafi, "And what about your medical problem?"

Rafi laughed nervously. "Somehow, I expected you to ask... that cleared up too, a couple of months ago."

[as heard from Rabbi Matisyahu Danziger, Bnei Brak]

A Chicken
for Shabbos

Rina Mizrachi* is a proud Sephardic woman who was born in Beit Shemesh, where she still lives today. She is proud of her Sephardic heritage and the fact that her great-granduncle was none other than the illustrious sage, Ben Ish Chai of Baghdad. She is proud of her five children who are all at the top of their classes in Yeshivos and Bais Yaakov schools. She is proud of the legacy of honesty and integrity that her late husband left after he passed away, almost six years ago. And she is most proud of being able to help support her family by working as a cleaning lady in other people's homes. But she is not at all proud of having found it necessary, at times, to accept *tzedakah*.

For the first few months after Rina's husband died, friends and neighbors voluntarily offered her money, food, and clothing to supplement her widow's benefits from the government. After a while, however, these acts of *chesed* gradually diminished as people began to forget about the quiet widow who never complained.

The domestic work did help to make ends meet during the week. But on Thursdays, Rina would be forced to decide between serving weekday food on Shabbos or going out to ask for assistance.

Rina always hoped that somehow her knocking on doors would not be necessary. Unfortunately, however, it almost always was necessary for her to go out on Thursday evenings to ask for help.

---

* All of the names in this story were changed by request.

Because she was so proud, Rina would never even think of collecting money in the street. And she never collected in her own neighborhood. Instead, she would travel to a different part of town each week, enter a building at random, and go from one apartment to the next.

Rina knew just how much she needed for the simplest Shabbos provisions. And whenever she had received what she needed for that week, she would stop collecting and go home. Maybe next week, she would think to herself, I won't need to go through this.

Most of the people Rina approached were quite generous. They were touched by this modest woman with weary eyes who asked for help for Shabbos. It never took Rina more than two hours to collect what she needed.

On Fridays, she would rise early and do all of her Shabbos shopping before going to work. That way she could begin cooking as soon as she came home.

✧   ✧   ✧

On that cold Thursday in January, Rina needed to go collecting, as usual. But this time, she found it much harder to get away from the house for two hours.

Rina's youngest child, seven-year-old Shimon, was in bed with a bad case of the flu, and he begged his mother not to leave. Even though Shimon's older sister, fourteen-year-old Miriam, was at home, Shimon wanted his mother. And who could blame him? He had fever and chills and really needed a mother's soothing presence.

As difficult as it was for Rina that night, she knew that if she did not leave the house to collect, there would be no Shabbos food that week. And how could she do that to the rest of the family? Maybe it won't take me so long tonight, she thought to herself, as she put on her coat and walked out the door.

On the way to the neighborhood where Rina had planned to seek assistance, she tried to think of what she could do to get back home as quickly as possible. Before she knocked on the first door, she came up with an idea. Instead of just asking for money, as she always did, she would ask for food. That way, she reasoned, she might not need to go to so many homes to get what she needed.

Rina's plan seemed to be working out as she had hoped. She had already collected some *challah*, fish, and an assortment of fruits and vegetables. Now comes the hard part, she thought. I still need a chicken. I cannot go home without a chicken, especially this week when the soup is so important for Shimon.

Rina knocked at the door of Mendel Sternberg, a full-time *kollel* student with eight children. Mendel's wife was out shopping so he left the *sefer* he was studying and answered the door.

"Please," Rina began, "could you help me for Shabbos? I am a widow with five children at home. Could you, by any chance, spare a chicken for Shabbos? If you could, I would be most grateful to you."

Mendel thoughtfully considered Rina's request. He did, in fact, have two chickens in his freezer. If he gave one to Rina, however, he would not have enough for his own family. He would then have to buy another one before Shabbos, but he really could not afford to do that. His own budget was stretched so thin already that he simply did not have enough money to buy another chicken this week.

Mendel deliberated with the prudence of a supreme court judge. He had no doubt that Rina's cause was legitimate. He definitely believed the story of this sincere, forlorn widow. But how could he deprive his own family of their needs? Regrettably, he decided that his own family must come first.

"I can give you a small donation," Mendel said, apologetically, reaching for his wallet. "But I am sorry that I am unable to give you a chicken."

Rina, thinking of Shimon waiting for her at home, decided to press her case further.

"Please, sir. I have a sick child at home with temperature, who really needs some chicken soup. If you could find it in your heart to give me a chicken, you would be granting him a *refu'ah shelemah*, a complete recovery, in addition to granting our family a decent Shabbos."

Mendel's brow furrowed deeply. He thought of the shoes his nine-year-old daughter needed, which he could not afford. He thought of the cracked window in his bedroom, which needed to be repaired. And he thought of the glasses he was told his five-year-old son would need, soon.

He didn't have the money for those necessities now. If he had to buy another chicken the next day, he'd be even further away from affording those items.

"I'm terribly sorry, Madam. But I am just not able to give you a chicken today. Perhaps, with Hashem's help, I will be able to give you a chicken some other time. But today, I just cannot do it."

Rina could sense Mendel's empathy and it gave her the encouragement to continue. Who knows if I will find anyone else as sympathetic as this man, she thought. She decided to try, again... one last time.

"Please, sir, forgive me for being so persistent. But I have been out collecting for over an hour. I have been on my feet cleaning floors since seven o'clock this morning. I want to go home to my sick child. Please. Please help a widow... Please give me a chicken for Shabbos."

Mendel fidgeted nervously with the fringes of his *tzitzis*. Tiny beads of perspiration appeared on his forehead as he glanced into the hall to make sure none of his neighbors were observing his predicament. He took a deep breath while his thoughts flashed back and forth.

Mendel pictured in his mind his old-fashioned refrigerator with the door latch that sometimes got stuck. He imagined himself opening the door and then opening the freezer compartment which was always caked with ice. He could clearly visualize the two frozen chickens his wife had purchased earlier that week.

Mendel's mind quickly shifted ahead to the pained expression which he imagined his wife would have, upon hearing about his generosity during her absence.

The next scene in Mendel's mind was the opened *sefer* he had just left, to answer the door. He remembered how comfortably engrossed in learning he had been before Rina had disturbed him so unexpectedly.

Rina was waiting patiently, with hopeful eyes, as Mendel wrestled with himself. Her presence, standing in his doorway, drew his mind back to the dilemma at hand.

If he would agree to Rina's request, Mendel told himself, it would not be the first time his wife would have to creatively stretch one chicken to feed their family. If Hashem had granted Mendel the good fortune to possess two chickens that week, he thought, did he have the right to deny one to this needy woman? Finally, would his generous and kind-hearted wife really be so disapproving, as he had initially imagined?

Mendel reconsidered. "All right. Please come in and have a seat. I'll just be a minute."

Rina sighed with relief but her relief was mixed with shame. What a mother won't do for her children, she thought. She stepped inside the modest Sternberg home and sat down on a chair. How similar the apartment was to her own! She heard Mendel walk into his kitchen and open the latch of his refrigerator. Then she jumped up at the sound of a cry and a loud, chilling scream. She could not imagine what accident might have just occurred. Instinctively, she rushed into the kitchen.

There Rina's mouth dropped open as she saw Mendel comforting his whimpering two-year-old son, who had turned blue from the few moments he had been locked inside the refrigerator.

Somehow, little Chesky had climbed inside the refrigerator without anyone noticing. Because of the old-fashioned latch on the door, once he was inside he could not free himself. And the thick insulation of the door had completely muffled the sound of his weak cries for help. His father had thought he was asleep in bed.

Had Rina not come to the Sternberg home that night; and had she not asked for a chicken for Shabbos; and had she not persisted; and had Mendel not relented and finally agreed to give Rina a chicken; and had he not gone over to open the refrigerator door just when he did, then...

Mendel had decided to do an act of *chesed* and, as a result, ended up saving the life of his own child.

[as heard from Rabbi Zev Jacobs,
Ramat Shlomo, Yerushalayim]

A Moving Story

Rabbi Akiva Solomon* is a well-known author, dynamic public speaker, beloved *Rosh Kollel* and Torah educator in Yerushalayim. He lives with his gracious wife, Rebbetzin Devorah, and their delightful children in the Sanhedria Murchevet neighborhood which, although teeming with many Torah scholars, still recognizes the unique spiritual asset of having Rabbi Solomon as a resident.

While Rabbi Solomon has achieved world-wide prominence today in the field of Jewish education, he was not always so well-known. Thirty years ago, as a single student learning in Yeshivah, he was considered just another *bachur*.

It was during that time that the young Reb Akiva dated Bracha Schiff. The match had been proposed by a local Rebbetzin who knew both parties.

"He's a young *talmid chacham*," the Rebbetzin had told Bracha before the two met. "You'll see — he'll become famous one day."

To Akiva she had said, "Bracha is a lovely girl with exceptional *middos*. And her father owns a successful moving business so you won't have to worry about finances."

Bracha and Akiva did meet, but for reasons which Rabbi Solomon cannot even remember today, he decided that Bracha was not the right match for him. He informed the Rebbetzin of his decision and that was that.

---

* All of the names in this story have been changed by request.

Many years later, Rabbi Solomon and his family were living in the Ezras Torah section of Yerushalayim. As their needs grew together with the size of their family, the Solomons contemplated the purchase of a new gas stove.

Now, to a *kollel* couple like the Solomons, a new stove can be a major expense, and the cost stretched their budget to the maximum. They deliberated extensively before finally deciding on the make and model of their choice.

Deciding which stove to buy was only one of many decisions the Solomons had to make. Where to purchase the stove was at least as important, if not more so. After checking with friends and neighbors, the Solomons discovered that they would get the best deal by ordering the American stove they wanted directly from the United States and having it shipped to Israel.

Much of the transatlantic correspondence between the Solomons and their parents in the States revolved around the purchase of the new stove. Finally, it was bought by Rebbetzin Solomon's parents and sent by ship to Israel. Five weeks later, the stove arrived at the port of Haifa.

Within the week, the Solomons received a written confirmation of the stove's arrival. Rebbetzin Solomon was delighted when she opened the envelope, and she couldn't wait to tell her husband.

Later that evening, after giving his *shiurim,* learning with his children, completing his own private fixed time for learning, and taking the innumerable phone calls from a wide array of petitioners, Rabbi Solomon sat down in the kitchen with his wife for a late-night glass of herbal tea.

"And how was *your* day?" Rabbi Solomon asked as he sipped his tea. "I've been so busy today, I'm not even sure I said 'Good morning' to you. I suppose it's too late for that now. But I'm not ready to say 'Good night' so let me hear about your day."

"I was pretty busy today, too," his wife said, laughing. "Of course, I'm not complaining but I spent over three hours this morning helping Mrs. Jacobowitz upstairs start cleaning for Pesach. She's been so worried about it since she broke her leg, that I thought I'd help her a little."

"You're unbelievable! As if you didn't have enough of your own work, you're always looking to help others." Rabbi Solomon beamed with pride. "What a *ba'alas chesed* you are."

Somewhat uncomfortable with the compliment, Rebbetzin Solomon changed the subject. "I'll bet you haven't seen the mail today. Do you know what we received?"

"No. Did we win the lottery?"

"Well, almost. Our stove arrived in Haifa."

"Fantastic! Now we'll have it in time for Pesach so you won't have to clean the old one."

"I wouldn't even mind cleaning the old one if I could rely on it to work," Rebbetzin Solomon laughed. "*Baruch Hashem* we've come this far. But now we have to figure out how to get it here. It's surely too big to pick up by car. Maybe we should rent a truck and ask some of the *bachurim* from the Yeshivah to go with you?"

Rabbi Solomon got up and adjusted one of his children's drawings on the refrigerator. Then he turned to his wife. "No," he said. "We wouldn't want a bunch of Yeshivah guys trying to carry the stove. That's all we need! I think we're probably better off with a professional moving company."

"Sounds like a good idea," the Rebbetzin agreed. "But I certainly wouldn't want to use the people who moved us last year. They broke too many things."

Rabbi Solomon finished his tea and rinsed out the glass. "I just thought of something! Tell me if this sounds crazy to you — I once went out with a girl whose father owns a moving company here. Maybe we should give him a call?"

"Why not? I'm sure you left things on good terms with the family. What have we got to lose? Give me the name and I'll look up the number and call them tomorrow. I don't want you to have to bother. You might feel uncomfortable and I don't want you to take away any time from your learning."

"See what I said about your being a *ba'alas chesed*?" her husband said gently. "You even do *chesed* to your husband —

now that's something special!"

Rebbetzin Solomon made the necessary calls and arrangements for Schiff Movers to transport the stove from Haifa to Yerushalayim. The price was agreed upon and delivery was promised in one to two weeks. Mr. Schiff explained that the paperwork alone could take almost a week. And with his backlog of deliveries, it could take as much as a whole second week before the stove would be delivered. But even if the stove arrived at the latest estimated date, it would still give the Solomons three weeks before Pesach to have it installed.

Rebbetzin Solomon was looking forward to using her new stove to cook and bake for Pesach. Since it was so close to *Yom Tov*, she planned not to use it for non-Pesach cooking so she would not have to clean it for Pesach.

In order to be fully prepared for the long-awaited new arrival, the Solomons decided to have their old stove removed in advance. A plumber came to disconnect the old stove and some *bachurim* from the Yeshivah volunteered to drag the worn-out antique down to the storage room in the basement. They only dropped the stove twice on the way downstairs but that made Rabbi Solomon all the more satisfied with himself for hiring a professional moving company to deliver his new stove.

Meanwhile, Rebbetzin Solomon managed with a small hotplate. It was quite an inconvenience, to say the least, but she was happy to put up with it since she knew it would be only for a short while...or so she thought.

The two weeks came and went without any word from Schiff Movers. By the end of the third week, even the usually patient Solomons were getting edgy.

Rabbi Solomon suggested that they call Mr. Schiff to see what was causing the delay. After all, Pesach was practically around the corner. In an another week, at the latest, Rebbetzin Solomon would need to have the stove installed so she could begin cooking for *Yom Tov*.

"Let's give it another week," she suggested. "He knows we need it before Pesach because I specifically mentioned that to him — so there must be some unavoidable delay. Let's try to give Mr. Schiff the benefit of the doubt."

"I don't know how you can be so calm about this," Rabbi Solomon replied. "I'd also like to be *dan l'chaf zechus,* but if we wait a full week, that will bring us to just three days before Pesach! Then we'll have to find someone to install it before you can even start cooking. You'll be under tremendous pressure — and what if it doesn't even arrive in a week? What will we do then?"

"I'm sure we'll manage," Rebbetzin Solomon said softly. "Let's wait and see."

Three days before Pesach, Rabbi Solomon's worst fears were being realized. The stove had not arrived and they had not even heard from Schiff Movers. Rabbi Solomon was fit to be tied.

"I knew I should have called earlier," he reprimanded himself during breakfast. "He's probably taking advantage of us because we're not bothering him. He's probably delivering other people's things instead of ours because we're being so patient!"

"We can't be sure of that, Akiva," Rebbetzin Solomon offered in defense of the moving company.

"But why else would the stove not have arrived? I could have practically *carried* it to Yerushalayim by now. I just can't imagine what is taking so long."

Rabbi Solomon began to pace the floor nervously. "And you know what else?" he said, more to himself than to his wife. "I wouldn't be surprised if Mr. Schiff is even *deliberately* delaying our delivery because he wants to get back at me for not going out a second time with his daughter. Who knows?"

He continued to pace the floor with even greater intensity than before. Suddenly he stopped and announced to his wife, "That's it — I'm not waiting any longer. I've had it. I'm going to call Mr. Schiff and tell him to cancel the order. He's fired! We'll get another company to move the stove. Even if it arrives after Pesach, I don't care. I feel he's made a fool out of us. Where's that phone number? I'm going to call him right now!"

Rabbi Solomon reached for the phone while Rebbetzin Solomon reluctantly handed him the phone number.

"Wouldn't you know? There's no dial tone," Rabbi Solomon mumbled as he slammed down the phone in frustration. "I'll try again in a few minutes."

Half an hour later, there was still no dial tone. Rabbi Solomon was so eager to fire Schiff Movers that he decided to go next door and ask to use the neighbors' phone to make the call. "I don't want to put this off any longer!" he said.

But the neighbor's phone did not have a dial tone either. Not one to give up easily, Rabbi Solomon decided to walk to the corner and use a public phone. Lifting the receiver, Rabbi Solomon was almost expecting the public phone not to be working either — and it wasn't.

In fact, no one in the entire neighborhood had phone service that morning. The Solomons eventually learned that due to a technical problem at the main switching station, none of the phone lines in the neighborhood were working that day.

Since Rabbi Solomon's Yeshivah was already closed for the Pesach vacation, he had arranged to learn with his *chavrusa* in the shul across the street from his home. He did so, but every two hours, he took a break to come home and see if the phones were working so he could make the call to fire Mr. Schiff. But each time he tried, Rabbi Solomon found that the phones were still dead.

In the afternoon, phone service had not resumed and people in the neighborhood were talking of little else. Rabbi Solomon returned home after *Minchah* to help his wife with the Pesach cleaning. With each passing hour he got more and more frustrated that he could not make his call. By the end of the day, however, Rabbi Solomon had become so engrossed in checking through his children's toys for *chametz* that he did not discover that the phones were working.

When the doorbell rang, Rebbetzin Solomon went to see

who was there.

"Rebbetzin Solomon?" asked the tall middle-aged man with a heavy key chain dangling from his belt. "I'm Mr. Schiff. We have your stove here. Where would you like my workers to put it?"

As Rebbetzin Solomon led Mr. Schiff and his workers into her kitchen, Rabbi Solomon followed close behind in disbelief.

"Since it's so close to Pesach, I figured you might have a hard time finding someone to connect the stove, so one of my men will do that for you now... at no extra charge, of course," Mr. Schiff added.

Rabbi and Rebbetzin Solomon were speechless. They stood in the kitchen as their new stove was being installed and just stared.

Mr. Schiff anticipated their questions and volunteered the answers. "I'm sure you're wondering why the stove wasn't delivered sooner, as I promised, and why I never called to explain the delay."

The Solomons, still speechless, nodded.

"The paperwork in Haifa was completed in less than a week and I even thought I'd get the stove to you before the date I promised." Mr. Schiff began. "But when my men came to pick it up, they couldn't find it! I even went to Haifa myself to try and locate it.

"It seems that someone accidentally moved it to another warehouse. You can imagine I was frantic trying to track it down — I had the papers to prove it had arrived but no one could tell me where it was.

"I didn't want to call you because I just didn't know what to say. I didn't think you'd be too thrilled to hear that your stove was lost! So I just kept trying to find it and finally succeeded.

"I knew you needed it for Pesach — so when I finally found it early this afternoon, I dropped everything and came straight back to Yerushalayim just to deliver it to you personally. I'm really sorry it took so long — but I'm glad you'll have it installed now at least two days before *Yom Tov*."

Looking back today, many years later, Rabbi Solomon still shakes his head at the *hashgachah pratis* involved. "If the phones had not been down in the entire neighborhood," he says, "I would have made a terrible fool of myself. Imagine — if I had been able to reach Mr. Schiff by phone, I would have angrily fired him. Not only would we have never gotten our stove for that Pesach, but what would have been far worse is that I would have insulted Mr. Schiff by unfairly blaming him. Here he was, up in Haifa, knocking himself out trying to locate our stove and I had judged him so unfavorably.

"When he arrived with the stove on the very day I was trying to fire him, all I could think was, *Baruch Hashem* the phones were not working! *Baruch Hashem* the phones were not working! As a result, I was saved from hurting Mr. Schiff and embarrassing myself.

"Now, it is not that unusual that we don't get a dial tone here in Israel," Rabbi Salomon explains. "In those years especially, it happened from time to time. But I don't remember any other time that the phones went dead in the *entire neighborhood*. I'm sure many people were inconvenienced that day, but I, for one, was really saved... Boy, was I saved!"

[as heard from Rabbi Akiva Solomon,
Sanhedria Murchevet, Yerushalayim]

Seeing through the Smoke

While I was glad to be back in Israel in August, 1995, I barely took note of the familiar beautiful scenery along the road from Ben Gurion Airport to Yerushalayim. The focus of my attention during the forty-minute ride was on inner thoughts or conversation with my fellow passengers.

When our taxi passed the turnoff to Moshav Shoresh, however, about twenty minutes outside of Yerushalayim, all conversation stopped abruptly and my fellow passengers and I stared through the windows in shock.

On either side of the highway, as far as the eye could see in both directions, all of the trees were scorched. The once beautiful green forest which had been so much a part of the breathtaking ascent to Yerushalayim consisted of the blackened skeletons of hundreds and thousands of trees. All of the leaves were missing and for a moment it almost seemed as if this were a surreal black winter scene, but the August heat reminded us all that this was very much summertime.

When conversation resumed inside our taxi, it was about the forest fire that had devastated the area in July. We had all heard the news at the time, but seeing the aftermath up close was much more dramatic than hearing a small item announced on the radio just before the weather and traffic reports.

How had it started? How long did it last? What was it like to be here at the time? What was it like for those who live in the area? What was it like for those who live in Yerushalayim?

What follows is the perspective of one Yerushalayim family. Others might describe the events differently. But this is

96

their story, as corroborated by newspaper accounts and inter-
views with other eyewitnesses.

✧   ✧   ✧

Shmuel Ben David* gently tucked the priceless manuscript back into its
manila envelope and returned it to the safe. Shmuel had been
preparing a description of this manuscript which would be
included in an updated catalog of his family's Judaica collection that had been started originally by his grandfather.
Shmuel sighed with satisfaction and then decided to take a
break from his draining work with this family heirloom.

As he left his book-lined study and walked toward the
kitchen he first smelled the acrid odor of smoke. They must
be burning refuse in the valley again, he thought as he took
himself a cold drink from the refrigerator.

Walking out on his porch, Shmuel gazed across the valley
behind his home in the Bayit Vegan neighborhood of Yerushalayim, looking for the garbage fire he expected to see. There
was no fire. Instead, he saw an unusual haze in the sky.

Before he could come to any tentative conclusions, his
wife, Tova, returned from shopping. "Shmuel," she exclaimed
breathlessly, "do you know what's happening? There's a forest
fire right outside of Yerushalayim. The road to Tel Aviv has
been closed in both directions. I heard about it on the bus just
now. Quick, let's turn on the radio — it's almost time for the
2:00 PM news."

Shmuel and Tova huddled over their radio as if they were
listening to civil defense instructions during an air raid. The
announcer's voice was solemn and somewhat shaky as he read
the news bulletin:

"A massive forest fire has broken out in the Jerusalem
corridor. It began about an hour ago near Moshav Shoresh.
The Jerusalem-Tel Aviv highway is closed to all civilian vehi-
cles; fire-fighting equipment is being rushed to the area. The

---

* All of the names in this story have been changed by request.

public is urged to stay as far away from the area as possible. Updates will be broadcast as they become available."

Shmuel and Tova ran outside to get another look at the darkening sky. Bits of soot were being swept along with the smoke that had already reached Yerushalayim. The strong summer winds were sweeping tangible evidence of the fire into the hot dry air, as if to corroborate the news broadcast they had just heard.

Other neighbors had also gathered outside to see the smoke for themselves. The gloomy expression on everyone's face showed that they all realized that this was no ordinary fire.

Tova's first thought was for the safety of her children. She mentally ran through the list assuring herself that none was out of town or anywhere near the blaze. Just to double check, she went back inside and called to make sure her married daughter, Leah, had not gone to visit a friend in the area. Shmuel then called his mother, who lived alone in the Givat Shaul neighborhood.

After a few more calls, they decided to turn on the radio again. The reporter sounded even more somber than before.

"The fire is blazing out of control. Initial efforts to contain it have failed. The Fire Department has called on the Air Force for helicopter assistance. Some workers have already suffered smoke inhalation and are being treated at the scene.

"All available Magen David Adom and volunteer ambulance personnel are requested to check with their bases immediately for instructions. All hospitals in the area have been put on emergency alert. The Army spokesman has announced that some evacuations may be necessary as a precaution."

Shmuel and Tova remained glued to their radio. They were soon joined by their two youngest daughters, Chaya and Batsheva, who returned home from school. They had been told of the fire by their teachers, who instructed them to run straight home and not to take any detours along the way. They burst in frightened and needed to be calmed down in between broadcasts.

"...Officials at the scene are acknowledging that they have never seen such a massive blaze. The high winds and recent above-average temperatures have created treacherous conditions. All efforts to contain the fire have been ineffective. Additional equipment and personnel are being rushed to the scene."

The Ben Davids did not panic as they listened to the frightening broadcasts. They had lived through many national crises since they had settled in Yerushalayim. Wars, terrorist attacks, and other emergencies taught them how to respond rationally, without undo fear. We didn't grow up like this, Tova thought to herself, as she reflected on her relatively calm childhood in Miami and Shmuel's in Paris.

Based on her experience with the most recent national emergency, the Gulf War, Tova knew that the first vital necessity that could become endangered was the water supply. Almost instinctively, she began filling empty bottles and jugs... just in case.

Shmuel went around the apartment and began closing the windows. From his living room, he could barely see through the smoke to the other side of the valley.

Back to the radio for more updates.

"... Residents of Kiryat Telshe Stone and the neighboring settlements are being evacuated. The evacuations are being slowed down by residents who are desperately trying to take valuables and other needed items with them. Preliminary reports indicate that as many as twenty homes in Shoresh have been damaged by the blaze. High winds continue to fan the inferno towards Yerushalayim. Flames are leaping as high as a hundred meters in the air and are interfering with the helicopters.

"The public is requested to keep as far away from the area as possible and to bring donations of blankets and clothing for the victims to the civil defense emergency stations in their locality. Officials at the scene have stated that the fire is still out of control, and that they have never seen anything like this in the entire history of the State."

✧   ✧   ✧

By the evening of July 2, the fire was finally contained. An estimated two million precious trees had been destroyed. Over thirty homes in Shoresh were engulfed in the wake of the worst forest fire Israel had ever seen.

Trees that had been planted almost fifty years before had gone up in smoke in one afternoon of terror. Dozens of frightened families had been displaced. Hundreds of other families had been forced to evacuate their homes temporarily, while thousands of others had feared for the safety of their own homes.

Even before the smoke cleared and the cleanup efforts began, spiritually sensitive people in Israel, like the Ben Davids, searched for meaning and lessons in these traumatic events.

Later that evening Shmuel and Tova felt so shaken up that they could not go to sleep easily. So they stayed up and tried to soothe their frazzled nerves with hot tea and reflective conversation.

"You know, Tova, this was a terrible tragedy, but we all have so much to be thankful for."

"You can say that again. If the fire had not been contained when it was, thousands of homes would have been destroyed instead of dozens."

"We must find out who is collecting funds for the victims. The least we can do is donate some money to help those whose homes were lost or damaged."

"Yes, that's a great idea. When you go to shul tomorrow, ask around and see if anyone knows who's collecting for the displaced families."

"Speaking of shul, tonight at *Ma'ariv* , someone mentioned to me that the fire stopped at the entrance to Kiryat Telshe Stone."

"That's very interesting. You know, it's surrounded by other communities that were very hard hit by the blaze. Why do you suppose it was spared?"

"Someone else pointed out that it has a Yeshivah. Perhaps

it was in the merit of the Torah study that went on there, that they were protected."

Our feet have stood firm [in battle, by the merit of the Torah studied]* at your gates, Yerushalayim.

TEHILLIM 122:2

[as heard from Shmuel and Tova Ben David, Bayit Vegan, Yerushalayim]

---

* See Rashi's commentary on this verse.

Rechov
Yaffo

The address is 180 Rechov Yaffo. Anyone familiar with the downtown area of Yerushalayim can recognize that this is far from the center of town. Traveling west on Rechov Yaffo, one passes the Central Post Office, the busy intersection at Rechov King George, and even the open-air market of Machane Yehuda well before reaching 180 Rechov Yaffo.

There is no store or office there. In fact there isn't even a door anywhere near the blue-and-white sign with the address. All that can be seen there are the corners of two one-story buildings and a narrow alleyway in between, leading back into an open courtyard. There are no signs on either side of the alley and people could pass it their entire lives without ever noticing it. But in spite of its unremarkable appearance, this alley opens into a unique world of intense human emotions.

Twice a week, from about 9:00 PM until the wee hours of the morning, literally hundreds of people from all over Israel come to wait outside of a small apartment adjoining the courtyard behind 180 Rechov Yaffo. Some are couples who are childless. Others are singles who need to find a *shidduch*. And still others are people whose relatives have been stricken with serious or life-threatening illness. What all these people have in common is that some tragedy in their lives has brought them to this address in search of a blessing from Rabbi Yona Levy.*

Rabbi Levy is a colorful and charismatic personality with a quick wit and a twinkle in his eye who attracts a following

---

* All of the names in this story were changed by request.

of both Israeli-born as well as foreign petitioners. His public lectures draw overflow crowds who enjoy his moral teachings spiced with plenty of humor and personal anecdotes.

As a Vizhnitzer *chasid*, Rabbi Levy is much more comfortable going to his Rebbe to receive a blessing rather than dispensing blessings himself. But many years ago, when he shared this discomfort with his Rebbe, Rabbi Levy was told, "If people are coming to you for blessings then it is a sign from Heaven that you should make yourself available. You must continue and you cannot turn people away."

In order to retain some semblance of family life, Rabbi Levy restricts his "office hours" to two nights a week. Initially, he was seeing people at his home on Rechov Yona in the Geula neighborhood of Yerushalayim, but eventually the crowds became so large that he was forced to find another meeting place.

One evening, before the relocation, Rabbi Levy was delayed and arrived home only after a long line had formed outside his second-story apartment. As he sheepishly made his way up the two flights of outdoor steps leading to his apartment, someone stopped him.

"Hey, where do you think you're going?" a young man confronted Rabbi Levy.

"I'm just going up to the second-floor apartment," Rabbi Levy replied matter-of-factly.

"Yeah? Well, so are all the rest of us. And we've been waiting here since before you came — there's a long line, you know. So why don't you go back down to the bottom of the stairs and wait your turn?"

It suddenly dawned on Rabbi Levy that this young man did not recognize him because it was his first visit. "What did he expect to find?" Rabbi Levy chuckles while recounting this episode. "He must have expected 'Rabbi Levy' to be an old man with a long white beard. Boy, was he surprised to learn that *I* was Rabbi Levy. I hope he wasn't disappointed!"

As an energetic man in his mid-fifties with a reddish beard, Rabbi Levy does not appear to fit the image of a Rabbi who dispenses blessings to hundreds of people each week. Nevertheless, he is the one for whom crowds of desperate, dispirited people wait patiently, hoping for the chance to spend a few precious minutes with him and receive his blessing or advice.

The following account is but one of the thousands of cases which have come to Rabbi Levy during his "office hours" at 180 Rechov Yaffo.

✧   ✧   ✧

It was a hot night in July when Rivka's turn finally came to meet with Rabbi Levy. The bus ride from Petach Tikvah had taken longer than she expected, so that by the time she arrived and signed her name, she was number 57 on the waiting list.

Would it really be worth all of this effort, she had asked herself as she sat in the poorly ventilated waiting room. But, then again, if even *half* of the stories she had heard about Rabbi Levy were true, it would definitely warrant the effort and the time.

When her name was finally called, Rivka haltingly entered Rabbi Levy's inner room and sat down across from his small desk. The desk was empty except for a large *Sefer Tehillim* and a telephone. A picture of the late Baba Sali, Rabbi Yisrael Abuchatzera, *zatzal*, hung on one wall and a large clock hung on the other.

Rabbi Levy asked Rivka where she was from and what she needed.

"I live in Petach Tikvah and I need a blessing for a *shidduch*."

In the brief conversation that followed, Rabbi Levy learned that Rivka had been divorced two years before and lived alone with her two small children. She received some child support from her former husband and supplemented that with her income as an elementary school teacher. She had been looking to remarry ever since she got divorced, but so far she had been unsuccessful.

In summing up her situation, Rivka said, "I need a husband. And my children need a full-time father." Then she took a handkerchief from her purse and wiped away a small tear from the corner of her eye.

Rabbi Levy closed his eyes and held his clenched right fist in the air. "May Heaven have mercy and assist you in finding a proper *shidduch* very soon," he declared.

Rivka whispered, "Amen. Thank you," and then left.

Two days later, Rabbi Levy returned to 180 Rechov Yaffo for his second time that week. The crowd of people waiting for him was just as large as it had been two days earlier. The hot weather doesn't seem to deter anyone, he thought to himself as he met with one petitioner after another.

It was close to midnight when Yehuda's turn came. A tall, good-looking man in his thirties, Yehuda entered Rabbi Levy's room with obvious respect. After he was told to sit down, he did not begin speaking until Rabbi Levy asked where he was from.

"I live here in Yerushalayim now, in the Beis Yisrael neighborhood."

"And how can I help you?" Rabbi Levy prompted.

"I need a blessing for a *shidduch*. I have been looking, but have not found anyone suitable... I suppose I should also mention that I was married before."

"How long ago did you get divorced?" Rabbi Levy asked, without thinking too much about it.

"Two years ago," came the reply.

Rabbi Levy sat up in his chair, jolted by a sudden thought. Could it be, he mused, that this is the ex-husband of the divorced woman who came to see me two nights ago? The possibility seemed very far-fetched. Nevertheless, Rabbi Levy studied his petitioner closely and decided to ask a few pointed questions. "Uh, tell me, Yehuda, where did you live when you were married?"

"We lived in Petach Tikvah, but after the divorce I needed a change so I moved to Yerushalayim."

"Do you have any children?"

"Yes. Two beautiful children," Yehuda's voice wavered. "I visit them once a week...but I think of them constantly."

"Does your ex-wife work now, or does she stay home and

care for the children?"

"No, she works too."

"What kind of work does she do?" Rabbi Levy asked, trying to conceal his mounting interest.

"She teaches fifth grade."

Rabbi Levy leaned back in his chair and closed his eyes. What unbelievable *hashgachah pratis*, he thought. This must surely be the ex-husband of the woman who came to see me only two days ago! That they are both looking to remarry is not at all unusual. But that they should both decide to come to me for a blessing in the same week is most extraordinary. This must be a sign to me from Heaven.

Rabbi Levy kept his eyes closed, raised his clenched right fist and announced, "May Heaven have mercy and assist you in finding a proper *shidduch* very soon."

Yehuda said, "Amen," softly, and then got up to leave.

"Just one moment, please. You said that you see your children once a week?"

"Yes, that's right. Why?"

"Do you go to your ex-wife's home to pick them up?"

"Yes, I do."

"Then when you visit them this week, please do me a favor."

"Of course — what is it?"

"Please give a message to your ex-wife for me. Please tell her that I would like to meet with you both. There is something that I would like to tell her in your presence. Do you think you could possibly come to see me, again, together with her?"

"Certainly, Rabbi. I will arrange it next week, *b'ezras Hashem*."

As promised, one week later, Yehuda returned to 180 Rechov Yaffo together with Rivka. They patiently waited their turn to see Rabbi Levy.

When Yehuda and Rivka were seated in the inner room, Rabbi Levy turned to Yehuda and asked, "Tell me, are you by any chance a *kohen*?"

Perhaps I should have asked him this question before, Rabbi Levy thought to himself as he waited quietly for Yehuda's answer.

Understanding that *kohanim* are not allowed by Jewish law to remarry their ex-wives, Yehuda realized why Rabbi Levy had asked this question. "No, I'm not a *kohen.*"

Rabbi Levy took a deep breath and placed both hands on the desk in front of him. "I'm sure by now you've figured out that you both came to see me last week, albeit on different nights."

Yehuda and Rivka nodded in silence.

"And I'm sure you must have realized by now how unlikely it is that you both just 'happened' to come to me the same week — with the same request," Rabbi Levy continued.

"I must tell you both that I see that 'coincidence' as a sign from Heaven. Look, I do not know either one of you very well, but you both impressed me as being special, sensitive and caring people."

Yehuda and Rivka stole brief glances at each other and then quickly turned away in embarrassment after their eyes met.

Rabbi Levy leaned back in his chair and smiled. Then he asked, "Do you realize that it is a great mitzvah for a divorced couple to remarry? I would like to propose to you both that you consider doing just that. Of course, I have no idea what it was that caused you to divorce, but whatever it was, I don't believe it is so serious that it should prevent you from remarrying. Any marriage takes work, and I believe that you are both willing to make your marriage work."

Rabbi Levy stopped to let his words sink in. "And, finally," he added, "let's not ever forget that there are two beautiful, sad children at home, who desperately need an Imma *and* an Abba."

Rivka took a handkerchief from her purse and wiped away a tear that was running down her cheek. Yehuda coughed nervously.

"Please take my suggestion seriously," Rabbi Levy concluded. "You both came to me asking for a blessing to find a *shidduch.* I truly believe that you are suitable for each other. The decision is surely up to you — but I feel that if you do get remarried, it will work out well. Let me hear good news from you both."

Rabbi Levy meets so many people each week that he cannot possibly remember each one. So when Yehuda telephoned a year later, it took a while for Rabbi Levy to recall who Yehuda was.

"We took your advice, Rabbi. We were married about two months after we met together with you in Yerushalayim."

"Oh, that's wonderful! Since you're still within the first year I can wish you *Mazal Tov!*"

"Rabbi, you can wish us another *Mazal Tov.* Rivka just gave birth to a baby boy. The *bris* will be next Friday, *b'ezrat Hashem.* We would like very much to honor you with being the *sandak.* After all, if not for you, this baby never would have been born."

"I am delighted to hear your news, Yehuda, and honored by your invitation. I would like to accept, but unfortunately, I'm just too busy now to be able to travel out of town on Friday. Please tell Rivka how happy I am that you called with such good news. *Mazal Tov* again, and all the best."

Two hours later, Yehuda called back. "Rabbi Levy, I've just made dozens of calls back and forth to my family and Rivka's family. Rivka and I just cannot think of having anyone else except you as *sandak* at our son's *bris.* So Rivka came up with the idea of having the *bris* in Yerushalayim so you can attend — we had to clear it with our relatives first, but they've all agreed to come to Yerushalayim just so you can be the *sandak.* I've already contacted a caterer and I'm only calling to inform you of the time and place."

"But how can you all manage to come to Yerushalayim on an *Erev Shabbos?*"

"Rabbi, if we have to stay over in Yerushalayim for Shabbos, we'll arrange that too! We simply must have you as the *sandak.*"

That Friday morning Rabbi Levy attended the *bris* and served as *sandak*, as Yehuda and Rivka had wanted. Both sets of grandparents were delighted to meet him and thank him personally for bringing their children together again.

Friday night, Rabbi Levy was still glowing. At the Shabbos table, he told his family all about the couple who had come to see him separately the year before. He especially wanted his family to appreciate the *hashgachah pratis* involved in Yehuda's and Rivka's independently deciding to come to him only two days apart from each other.

...And, I suppose, it was also *hashgachah pratis* which was responsible for my having been a guest at Rabbi Levy's home on that Friday night when he told this story.

[*as heard from Rabbi Yona Levy,*
Geula, Yerushalayim]

The Hotel Room

Well before the El Al B-747 touched down at Ben Gurion Airport, all members of the cabin crew learned that Sylvia Kent* thought she must always get her way. During the long flight from Johannesburg, South Africa, Sylvia had requested three times that her seat be changed.

The first time was even before takeoff, when Sylvia decided that she was sitting too close to the smoking section. A stewardess quickly canvassed the passengers and found one who volunteered to trade places.

The second time was less than two hours later, when Sylvia insisted that she could not continue to sit directly behind a cranky two-year-old. Another stewardess was less enthusiastic about helping, but eventually did manage to negotiate seat-swapping for Sylvia.

The third time Sylvia requested a seating change she complained that her seat was too close to the bathrooms. It was then that the cabin crew refused to accommodate her. Not one accustomed to acquiescing, Sylvia took the refusal as a declaration of war. She raised her voice, insisted on speaking with the Chief Steward, and threatened a variety of retaliatory actions, all to no avail.

Sylvia's disembarking of the El Al plane stirred a mixture of intense emotions. The cabin crew were greatly relieved to see Sylvia finally leave the plane. They were practically elated. On the other hand, the rest of her fellow tourists on the

---

* All of the names in this story have been changed by request.

two-week Five Star Tour of Israel, were most apprehensive about how Sylvia's disposition might interfere with their vacation.

For most of the other 43 members of the Five Star Tour, this was their first trip to Israel. For that reason they had chosen a tour that promised to take care of all meals, hotel accommodations, and sightseeing for the entire two weeks. This was in January, 1975, which is the middle of the summer vacation season for those who live in the southern hemisphere.

Since few of the members of the tour were Jewish, Sylvia was not the only non-Jew. And while many of the tourists were couples in their fifties and sixties, Sylvia was not the only single person in her forties. But by the time the tour group checked in to their first hotel, everyone knew that Sylvia was the most outspoken member of the group... to say the least.

The first three days of the tour were spent sightseeing and shopping in and around Tel Aviv. The next two days were spent in and around Haifa. Another three days were filled traveling through the Galil and returning each night to the same hotel in Tiberias.

The members of the tour group were scheduled to spend the remainder of their time in Yerushalayim, while staying at the King Solomon Hotel.

As the bus approached Yerushalayim, Uri, their Israeli guide, turned on his microphone to address the members of the tour.

"Soon we shall be entering the holy city of Jerusalem. Although the name of the city means peace, it is a city over which more wars have been fought than any other city in the history of the world. We shall be spending the rest of our trip here because there is so much to see: the museums, the holy places, and the archeological excavations. When we are through, you will understand why we have saved Jerusalem for the last — and best — part of our tour.

"We will be going first to our hotel, the King Solomon.

There we will check in and spend about two hours unpacking and getting settled. Then we will be going out to the Old City of Jerusalem. We will be going to the holy sites in all parts of the Old City: the Armenian Quarter, the Christian Quarter, the Moslem Quarter, and finally, the reconstructed Jewish Quarter.

"We will visit the Jewish Quarter last because we want to be there at sundown, which is the most interesting time to visit the famous Western Wall. Religious Jews come to the Wall at sundown to pray. It is also the time when some brides and grooms come to the Wall to be photographed on the day of their wedding.

"There is much more I can say about the Wall but we should wait until we are standing there."

Sidney Fink, a retired accountant, called out from the back of the bus, "Uri, could you just tell us, is it called the 'Western Wall' or the 'Wailing Wall'?"

Uri switched the microphone back on and blew into it to make sure it was working. "The answer, Mr. Fink, is that it is called *both* the 'Western Wall,' and the 'Wailing Wall.' The name 'Western Wall' refers to the fact that it is the Western retaining wall of Herod's enlargement of the Temple Mount, and a remnant of the Temple complex that was destroyed by the Romans in 70 CE. The name 'Wailing Wall' refers to the fact that for almost two thousand years, Jews have been coming there to pour out their hearts in prayer and weeping."

Helen Gold, a proud grandmother who was constantly displaying snapshots of her grandchildren, raised her hand. "Uri, could I just ask one more question, please?"

"Of course, Mrs. Gold," Uri obliged.

"Why is there so much praying at the Wall and not at a synagogue?"

"The Wall *is* a synagogue, even though it does not have a roof. There are arks with Torah scrolls there, prayer books, and everything that you would find in a synagogue in South Africa. But that is not the complete reason. The Temple Mount is the most holy place in all of Judaism and this is as close as we are permitted to come. According to tradition it is the mountain where Abraham bound Isaac on the altar and also the site of Jacob's dream. It is the exact spot where Solomon's Temple stood.

"According to Jewish tradition, it is the place where all prayers enter the gates of Heaven. When you get to the Kotel, you will see little pieces of paper stuck in between the cracks. These are written prayers that people have left in the Wall. According to Jewish tradition, prayers placed in the Wall are more likely to be answered. There are many recent stories of both Jews and non-Jews who have had their prayers at the Wall answered, miraculously."

Helen nodded. "Thank you so much, Uri."

A few minutes later, the tour bus pulled into the circular driveway of the King Solomon Hotel.

Two-and-a-half hours after the tour group had arrived at the King Solomon Hotel, all of the South African tourists were seated on the bus — except one. Uri nervously glanced at his watch as he muttered to himself, "I think I'll just have to go in, again, and get her."

Before he could get off the bus, an irate Sylvia emerged from the hotel lobby, followed close behind by a most contrite hotel manager.

"Ms. Kent, I am terribly sorry — please believe me. We are already overbooked though, and there is nothing I can do about it. Please let us make it up to you another way," begged the manager.

Sylvia turned on her high heels, facing the manager, as the two stood alongside the tour bus. "I've already told you that I do not like the room I've been given. It is simply unacceptable. Throughout this tour, there has been one foul-up after another, but until now at least the hotel rooms were decent. There is absolutely no way I will stand for this. Do you understand?!"

"Yes, of course I understand your disappointment. And I am terribly sorry you are so dissatisfied. But at this point, there are no other rooms available at all. I cannot just kick someone else out of their room and force them to exchange with you. And I can't give you a room I do not have," reasoned the manager.

"Look," Sylvia shouted, waving her finger in the manager's face, "that's *your* problem. I insist on having another room and that's what I expect to get. I have no intention of staying in the room I have now."

"Ms. Kent!" Uri cut in. "Everyone is waiting for you. You can continue to 'discuss' this matter with the hotel manager when we return. But you have already kept the entire bus waiting for over half an hour."

"Uri, this delay isn't my fault, you know," Sylvia barked as she climbed into the bus and took her seat. "If they had simply given me a decent room, I would have been out here way ahead of everyone else."

During the short bus ride to the Old City, Sylvia continued to stew about her room assignment. Adopting a softer tone, she succeeded in winning some sympathy from her fellow tourists.

"I don't blame you for being upset, Sylvia," Helen commiserated. "I was pretty annoyed in Haifa when they told us they didn't know anything about Norman's salt-free diet. After all, what did they expect him to do? Just skip supper? I wouldn't exactly give this tour five stars, either."

"I have an idea, Sylvia," chimed in Sidney. "Why don't you write out a prayer for a better room and place it in the Wall when we get there?"

A number of other passengers overheard the conversation and added their support for Sidney's suggestion.

Sylvia dismissed the idea immediately. "I'm not even Jewish. Why should my prayer be answered?"

"But Uri said that prayers of both Jews and non-Jews are answered at the Wall," Sidney countered.

By the time the bus arrived at the Old City, the entire bus full of tourists was trying to convince Sylvia to write out a prayer for a new room at the hotel and stick it in the Wall. Bowing to the pressure of the group, she agreed. But in order to still feel in control, she mockingly set it up as a test.

"Okay, I'll do it," Sylvia announced as the bus parked. "But this will be an opportunity to prove whether Jewish tradition is correct... and whether Uri is really a licensed tour guide!"

Just as Sylvia had a knack for getting on people's nerves, she also knew how to liven up the otherwise lifeless group. Her wisecracks and jokes were especially welcomed on some of the longer bus rides during the tour. Now she was once again sparking laughter among the group.

"Perhaps this will earn me a place in the *Guiness Book of Records*," Sylvia boasted. "I can just see it: 'First person to disprove two-thousand-year-old Jewish tradition regarding the Western Wall...'"

At the women's section of the Wall, surrounded by at least a dozen of her fellow tourists, Sylvia ceremoniously placed her written prayer between the cracks of the Wall. When she returned to the bus, everyone wanted to know if she had "done it."

"I'll be holding a press conference as soon as Uri gives me his microphone," Sylvia announced.

While the bus drove back to the hotel, Sylvia fielded questions from her audience. "Yes, I did write out a prayer for a better room at the King Solomon Hotel, and I placed it in the Wall. But unless there is really any validity to that tradition about prayers being answered, the King Solomon Hotel is going to face one heck of a law suit," Sylvia mocked, to the amusement of her fellow tourists.

As the Five Star Tour bus pulled into the circular driveway of the King Solomon Hotel, before the bus even stopped, the hotel manager burst out of the lobby with a euphoric look on his face.

"Ms. Kent!" he shouted. "Ms. Kent! I must speak with you!"

Sylvia got up from her seat and slowly made her way to the door. No one else budged and no one made a sound. All eyes followed Sylvia Kent as she stepped toward the front of the bus and met the manager who jumped on board to greet her.

"You won't believe this, but we have a deluxe room for you! Someone checked out unexpectedly and now we can give you a better room. And this is not just any deluxe room — this is our only deluxe room with a view of the Old City."

For the first time on the tour... and maybe even in her life, Sylvia Kent was speechless.

As the two-week tour was drawing to a close, Helen and Norman Gold decided to extend their trip another week. They felt they wanted to spend more time in Yerushalayim.

During that additional week, they took Rabbi Yom Tov Cohen's Friday morning walking tour of the Old City (See "Missing Stones").

After the tour, they approached Rabbi Cohen and told him the miraculous story of how Sylvia Kent prayed for and received a better room at the fully booked hotel.

Then they asked Rabbi Cohen to explain to them why someone like Sylvia Kent should have such prayers answered, even if she did write them down and insert them in the Wall? Wasn't her request relatively unimportant? Wasn't she deriding Jewish tradition with her mockery? Was this a sincere prayer that was worthy of being answered so quickly?

Rabbi Yom Tov Cohen gave the Golds the following explanation:

When King Solomon built the Holy Temple in Yerushalayim, he knew that the beauty, majesty, and sanctity of the Temple would attract not only Jews, but non-Jews as well. He was concerned about safeguarding the honor of Heaven in the eyes of the non-Jews who would visit the Temple.

If Jews prayed at the Temple and their prayers were not answered, their belief in Hashem would not be diminished in any way. They would still feel that their prayers were heard and they would not regret their pilgrimage to Yerushalayim.

But if non-Jews came to the Temple to pray and their prayers were not answered, they might come to mock the sanctity of the Temple. Therefore, King Solomon offered a personal prayer upon the completion of the Temple: He asked that the prayers of non-Jews be answered *more* quickly than the prayers of Jews.

Rashi, in his commentary on *Melachim I* 8:43, explains why:

> Jews know Hashem and believe that He has the power to answer all prayers. So if a Jew's prayer is not answered, he will attribute it to his own unworthiness. But a non-Jew whose prayer is not answered will say, "The Temple, whose reputation encompasses the world and for which I have gone to such great effort to travel there and pray — now I see that it is worthless, just as all other religions are worthless." Therefore [King Solomon asked Hashem to grant] everything for which non-Jews pray.

Thus, even the most cynical non-Jew would leave the site of the Holy Temple with reverence for its sanctity... even a cynic like Sylvia Kent.

[as heard from Rabbi Yom Tov Cohen,
Ezras Torah, Yerushalayim]

On the
Beach

In August, 1982, a small, informal group of Rabbis in Eretz Yisrael requested that I meet with them to present psychological insights on dating, courtship, and marriage. What we had planned as a single meeting evolved into a series of three workshops throughout the month.

The following summer, I happened to be in Eretz Yisrael again and ran into Rabbi Zvi Kesser*, the principal organizer of the previous summer's workshops. He insisted that I allow him to reconvene the group so that I could address them again on the same subject. A date was set and calls were made, all with breathtaking spontaneity. "If you're here, again, this summer," Rabbi Kesser observed, "it is a sign from Heaven that our group must meet with you again."

One of the most enthusiastic participants at the gatherings in 1982 was Rabbi Zalman Glick. Not only did he attend all three workshops, but he was also the only participant who took notes in addition to tape-recording each session.

Rabbi Glick was especially interested in these meetings because, in addition to his teaching responsibilities at one of the local seminaries, he was also in charge of providing counseling to the students at two other institutions. He found the meetings, therefore, particularly relevant to his work.

Rabbi Glick eagerly attended the workshops. In fact, he was the first to arrive and the last to leave each session. I valued his participation at least as much as he valued the

---

* All of the names in this story were changed by request.

workshops. His questions and comments stimulated the entire group.

It is not difficult to understand, therefore, why I took it for granted that Rabbi Glick would attend the workshops in 1983. So I asked about him during one of the initial planning phone conversations with Rabbi Kesser. "I assume you will be inviting Rabbi Glick as well, won't you?"

"Unfortunately not," Rabbi Kesser replied apologetically. "I know he moved recently but I don't have his new phone number. He really should be invited, but I have no idea how to reach him. And I haven't even seen him around lately. But if there is any way you can get his number, I'll be glad to invite him."

The ball was in my court. But I had no leads whatsoever. We certainly could have met without him. He would have been extremely disappointed, though, if he learned of our gathering after the fact. Moreover, he had contributed so much in the summer before that I would very much miss his presence now. But I had no way to find him.

First, I tried his old number. That had been disconnected without any new number given. Next I tried Directory Assistance, but all they had was the old number. The one or two mutual acquaintances I tried could tell me only that they knew the Glicks had moved recently — but they could not tell me exactly where. As the date of the meeting grew closer, I even started looking for Rabbi Glick on every bus... all to no avail.

Eventually, I came to accept the fact that Rabbi Glick would not be included this time. My wife, however, was not as pessimistic. "You'll see," she reassured me. "One of us will end up meeting Rabbi Glick before your session with the *Rabbanim*. We always run into so many people in Israel when we need to find them even for unimportant reasons. So in this case, I have no doubt that he will turn up. A lot can happen in the next two days... just wait and see!"

I did not have as much *bitachon* as my wife. The next time I spoke with Rabbi Kesser, I told him, "I can't seem to locate Rabbi Glick either. Unless you should happen to bump into him, we'll just have to proceed without him."

✧   ✧   ✧

One of the many opportunities in Eretz Yisrael which are not available in New York is the chance to go swimming at a beach which has separate days for men and women. Since it was *bein ha-zemanim* and vacation time, Rabbi Kesser had gone to the beach earlier in the week with his two older sons. Now it was the ladies' turn, so Rabbi Kesser's wife, Esther, took their two younger children, six-year-old Dinah and two-year-old Yaakov, to the beach.

Although young boys are not allowed on the beach during women's days, no one objects to little boys under the age of three accompanying their mothers. Little Yaakov was still in pony tails, before having his first haircut.

Esther packed up the bathing suits, beach toys, and lunch and then headed out with Dinah and Yaakov in tow to wait for the chartered bus to the beach. Yaakov could not remember his last summer's trip to the beach and had no idea what to expect. His veteran beach-going older sister sagely prepared him for the excitement ahead. "There is so much sand there that you'll never run out of it. There's also shells and waves and if we're good, maybe Mommy will buy us ice cream!"

Esther, on the other hand, was much more subdued than her two traveling companions. She was thinking about needing to keep a constant eye on the two children. Going to the beach was not such a relaxing experience for mothers.

Yaakov and Dinah happily chatted to their mother and each other throughout the hour-long busride to the beach. Once there, Esther gave the following gentle but firm instructions:

"No matter where we go, we must always stay together, children. You can play in the sand, but you can't throw it! And don't go anywhere near the water without me."

Esther successfully negotiated the clothing changes and found a comfortable spot on the beach. Dinah was begging to go into the water, while all Esther wanted was to relax on the sand — and maybe even close her eyes.

Some heavy negotiating followed, with Dinah extracting a

compromise from her mother. The three would sit at the edge of the water, just where the waves came up to the beach.

Yaakov squealed with delight as each wave washed up to his toes, but he didn't want to get much closer than that. Dinah rolled in the water and gathered shells. Esther waded into the surf and enjoyed this rare and welcomed refreshment.

After a while, Esther could not resist the urge to go in for a real swim. She had prepared her children for this brief separation by explaining that she would look for a trustworthy adult to leave them with for about ten minutes.

Esther did, in fact, find a familiar face, a neighbor from the next building, who gladly agreed to watch Dinah and Yaakov while Esther went out further for an unencumbered swim.

"You could have stayed in longer if you wanted," the neighbor said when Esther returned.

"Thank you so much," Esther replied, "but I wouldn't want to take advantage of you. And anyway, I really want to just relax on the beach for a while now."

Esther took out the digging toys and announced that it was now time for Dinah and Yaakov to build themselves a sand castle. Dinah grabbed the toys and immediately assumed the role of construction foreman with Yaakov eagerly accepting the role of subordinate.

Esther rearranged a few things and settled down to relax a little. What a lovely day this has been, she thought as she adjusted herself comfortably.

The waves were hypnotically washing up onto the beach. The cool sea breeze was perfectly offsetting the strong Mediterranean sun. And the laughing voices all around blended in the background to add to the soothing atmosphere.

Esther glanced over to check once again on her busy children. "Where's Yaakov?" she asked, as much to herself as to Dinah.

Dinah reluctantly looked up from her digging. "He's right over... Hey, where is he?"

Esther had already jumped to her feet. Oh, this is just what I was afraid of! she thought.

"Wait right here and don't you dare move," Esther instructed Dinah. Then Esther raced the few yards to the water and scanned the surf. He couldn't have wandered into the water since he seemed so frightened of the waves, she reassured herself. But even if he had, surely someone on the crowded beach would have noticed. Then she raced back to Dinah.

"Come on, we've got to find Yaakov," she called, grabbing Dinah by the hand.

Running off at random, Esther and Dinah began to scour the beach, calling, "Yaakov? Yaaaakov!" Along the way, sympathetic women read the panic on Esther's face and in her voice and inquired what was wrong. Esther kept giving out descriptions of Yaakov, like a campaign worker handing out leaflets on the eve of an election.

Somehow, though, Esther was not so concerned for Yaakov's safety. In such a short amount of time, she reasoned, he probably could not get hurt. But since she and her husband wanted their children to learn English, they did not speak Hebrew at home. As a result, while Yaakov did speak full sentences, he hardly knew any Hebrew. So Esther worried that this would compound his fear as soon as he realized he was lost.

Frantically, Esther weaved her way through the crowded masses on the beach. She peered in every direction even while she was giving out Yaakov's description to anyone who seemed the least bit interested. He really could not have gone very far away, Esther told herself as she shielded her eyes from the sun.

As the seconds ticked away, Esther became more and more frantic. She felt herself wanting to run in all directions at once. Dinah even offered to search in another direction, but Esther was too frightened that Dinah, too, might get lost. What a nightmare this has turned into, Esther thought as she widened the circle of her search.

Finally, someone advised her to go to the lifeguard and ask her to announce a lost child from her microphone. "Even if your son doesn't speak Hebrew," Esther was told, "at least many more people will be alerted to his being missing. That's how I found my Avrumie when he wandered off last year."

Esther thanked the woman and headed off toward the lifeguard's tower with renewed hope. Now why didn't I think of this, she chided herself.

As Esther made her way toward the lifeguard's tower, she heard an announcement coming over the loudspeaker in Hebrew. "A small girl around two years old has been found. Will the mother please come to the lifeguard tower immediately."

That may be Yaakov! Esther thought. With his ponytails, the lifeguard might have mistaken him for a girl.

Esther told Dinah that she thought Yaakov had been found and the two quickened their steps to the tower. Esther's relief was mixed with apprehension as she imagined Yaakov crying in fear, surrounded by the strange lifeguards speaking a language he didn't understand.

Out of breath and panting, Esther and Dinah finally reached the lifeguard's tower. To Esther's surprise, she saw Yaakov giggling happily in the lap of a gentle lifeguard who was trying to entertain him until his mother arrived.

Esther called out to Yaakov who only looked up and smiled at his mother and sister. Obviously, he didn't even realize he had been lost.

Esther approached the lifeguard. "I was watching them constantly! I just don't know how the little one managed to wander off. Thank you so much," she gushed. "I'm so sorry to have bothered you."

"It was no bother at all," the lifeguard chuckled. "She's an adorable little girl. And you need not apologize — little kids wander off here all the time. Yours is the third one today! Anyway, you really don't have to thank *me*. I didn't find her."

"Then who did?" Esther asked.

"That woman over there, with the yellow hat and sunglasses. All *I* did was announce that she was found."

Esther then thanked the lifeguard and took Yaakov by the hand. Together with Dinah, they walked over to the woman in the yellow hat.

"Excuse me — the lifeguard said that it was you who found my son?" Esther asked in Hebrew.

"Yes," the woman in the yellow hat replied in English. "I saw him wandering around by himself and realized he must be lost."

"Oh, you're an American?"

"Yes, I'm originally from Queens but now I live in Yerushalayim. Are you living here or just visiting?"

"I'm originally from the States, too, and now we live in Yerushalayim, in Mattersdorf. My name is Esther Kesser. I really can't thank you enough. You know, he was there one minute and the next, he was gone."

"I know exactly what you mean. It's already happened to me, too. My name is Malka Glick."

"Oh, how funny! My husband has been trying all week to locate someone named Glick but he couldn't find his telephone number. You wouldn't, by any chance, be related to a Rabbi Zalman Glick, would you?"

"Why, uh, yes... He's my husband!"

So my wife was right, after all. Rabbi Glick did turn up, just as she had predicted.

Rabbi Glick was delighted to learn of the session the next evening and did attend... together with his notebook and tape recorder.

[as heard from Rabbi Zvi Kesser,
Kiryat Mattersdorf, Yerushalayim]

A Breath
of Hair

A thick fog enveloped the Bayit Vegan neighborhood of Yerushalayim early one Sunday morning in December, a few years ago. The damp winter wind blew through the still empty streets as Mirel Landau* shut off her alarm clock and pulled back the curtain of her bedroom window to peek outside.

A good day to stay in bed, she thought to herself as she overcame the urge to go back to sleep. She got dressed quickly and started *davening* right away so she wouldn't be late for her teaching job in the Ramat Eshkol neighborhood.

Mirel sat down to breakfast just as her father, Rabbi Menachem Landau, an administrator in Yeshivah Ore Ganuz, came home from shul. "Wow, is it cold out there!" he announced as he unwound the scarf from around his neck.

Joining Mirel in the kitchen, Rabbi Landau sat down next to her and cut a slice of bread from the loaf on the table. "This is a nice treat," he began cheerfully. "I don't often get the chance to have breakfast with you. Since this past Shabbos was an out-Shabbos for the Yeshivah, I don't have to be at work until 9:00 this morning."

Mirel gently tapped the shell of her soft-boiled egg and looked up at her father with a smile. "I'm also glad we can have breakfast together."

"Rachel, Gila, Yanky, you'd better get up now or you'll be late for school," Mrs. Landau called over her shoulder as she entered the kitchen. "Oh, Menachem!" she said, noticing her

---

* All of the names in this story have been changed by request.

husband, "how nice to have you with us for breakfast today."

Mrs. Landau sat down at the kitchen table and peeled back the tin foil lid of a yogurt container. Turning to Mirel, she said, "You know, I got a call last night from Rebbetzin Blau. She said that she met a wonderful boy from the Kesser Torah Yeshivah, who is eligible now. His family is from Kfar Chassidim — and his father is a *mashgiach* in the Yeshivah there. He's 23 — and she said he might be a good *shidduch* for you. What do you say, Mirel? Should we look into it further?"

Mirel dropped her spoon on her plate with a loud clink. "Oh, Imma, I'm so fed up with *shidduchim*! I know I'm only 21, but I've been out with so many boys already. I just don't have the patience anymore."

"But you do want to get married, don't you?" asked Rabbi Landau, somewhat alarmed by Mirel's reaction.

"Of course I do, Abba, but all this dating has taken its toll! Do you think it's easy to get dressed up each time, hoping that maybe this is 'the one,' only to see that I've wasted another evening. I'm just getting discouraged."

"Do you want me to tell Rebbetzin Blau that we're not interested?" Mrs. Landau asked softly.

"No...oh, I don't know!" Mirel replied in frustration.

Rabbi Landau slowly spread some jam on his bread. "Suppose," he said, "we just make a few inquiries...let's try to find out a little more about this young man. You can always decide not to meet him if you don't want to."

"Look, Abba, you know what I'm looking for in a boy," Mirel said. "We've discussed it so many times already. At this point, what I think I want is for you to meet the boy first. *You* talk with him and if you really think he's for me, then I'll agree to go out with him. But I'm not ready to meet him just on someone else's say-so."

"Fair enough," Rabbi Landau agreed, with some relief. "We'll do our checking and if he sounds suitable, I'll arrange to go to the Yeshivah and speak with him."

Mirel glanced at her watch and then gulped down the rest of her coffee. "I'd better *bentsch* now or I'll be late for work," she said, reaching for a *bentscher*.

Throwing on her coat, Mirel grabbed her briefcase and dashed for the door. Then she stopped short. "Abba," she blurted out breathlessly, "please don't forget what I told you last time. If you do meet the boy, make sure he doesn't have *peyos* hiding behind his ears! There's absolutely no way I would consider any boy with *peyos*."

Rabbi Landau smiled. He knew his daughter's likes and dislikes well.

Mrs. Landau called Rebbetzin Blau for more details about the young man, Yehoshua Mandel.

Rebbetzin Blau was delighted. "I've known your Mirel since she was a little girl," she said, "and I've only met Yehoshua once. But from what I've seen and heard about him, he seems to be just what Mirel is looking for!"

Later that evening Rabbi Landau called one of his old friends. "Aaron, how are you and how's the family?"

"*Baruch Hashem*, fine, Menachem. So nice to hear from you. To what do I owe the honor of your call?"

"Well, to get straight to the point, Aaron, I need a favor."

"Sure. For you, anything. How can I help you?"

"Are you still teaching at Kesser Torah? I need information about one of the *bachurim*. It's for a possible *shidduch* for my Mirel."

"No problem, Menachem. Who's the lucky boy who's being considered for the coveted position of son-in-law?"

"Aaron, please, cut the kibitzing. The boy's name is Yehoshua Mandel."

"Well, he's not in my *shiur*, but by tomorrow evening, I should be able to get all the information you need."

The next night, as promised, Aaron called Rabbi Landau with a full report. Yehoshua was in the second to highest *shiur* and was a serious Torah scholar. He was highly respected by his peers and Rabbis alike. Somewhat on the outgoing side, Yehoshua had a good sense of humor but also knew when and how to be serious.

"Aaron, he sounds like just what we're looking for. I don't

know how to repay you."

"No problem, Menachem. I'll tell you what you can do. When my daughter starts going out, if I have to check out a boy in Yeshivah Ore Ganuz, you can return the favor!"

Rabbi Landau laughed. "Aaron, it will be my pleasure."

As soon as Rabbi Landau got off the phone, he sat down with his wife and repeated the conversation.

"I suppose the next step would be for you to meet with Yehoshua yourself," Mrs. Landau said. "Maybe I should call Rebbetzin Blau and see how this can be arranged."

The following week, Rabbi Landau went to Yeshivah Kesser Torah at the prearranged time. He met Yehoshua in the empty lunchroom and the two went outside for a walk. They spoke about the *Gemara* Yehoshua was learning, the weekly Torah portion, and Israeli politics.

Twenty minutes later, they were back at the Yeshivah and said good-bye to each other. Yehoshua mentioned that his afternoon *seder* was about to start and he did not want to keep his *chavrusa* waiting. A considerate fellow, Rabbi Landau thought to himself, as the two shook hands.

Rabbi Landau waited on the sidewalk as Yehoshua turned to enter the Yeshivah. He wanted to get a good look at the back of Yehoshua's head. Perfect, he thought to himself, as he scrutinized the boy's head — no *peyos* at all!

A week later, Mirel and Yehoshua met each other for the first time. After so many disappointments, Mirel was not looking forward to the date. But when she walked in the door after Yehoshua brought her home, her face was more radiant than her parents had seen in a long time. Six weeks later, Mirel and Yehoshua were engaged. And the wedding took place two weeks before Pesach.

The young couple purchased an apartment in Kiryat Sefer and moved in the week after *sheva berachos*. Since the new couple spent Pesach with the Landaus in Bayit Vegan, they spent Shavuos with the Mandels in Kfar Chassidim.

For Sukkos, it was the Landaus' turn to host the young

couple. After the *seudah* of the first night of *Yom Tov*, Rabbi Landau came inside from the porch where his *sukkah* was located and sat down on the couch in the living room. Yehoshua also came inside and then excused himself, as he was going to the local Yeshivah to learn.

As Yehoshua turned to leave, Rabbi Landau noticed some unmistakable tufts of hair behind Yehoshua's ears. Rabbi Landau's eyes widened at the unexpected sight but he said nothing until Yehoshua left.

Mirel came into the living room and sat down. She told her father how happy she was with Yehoshua and how much she was enjoying married life in Kiryat Sefer.

Rabbi Landau listened with only half an ear. While Mirel was talking, he could not help wondering about the *peyos* he had unmistakably seen behind Yehoshua's ears! Should he ask about them or not, he wondered. On the one hand, maybe this was a sore point between the couple, and if so, why bring it up? On the other hand, Mirel seemed so happy with Yehoshua — so surely this must not bother her.

Rabbi Landau's curiosity won out and he decided to ask. Gingerly, he broached the topic with his daughter. "Uh, Mirel, when Yehoshua walked out just now, I, uh, couldn't help noticing the, um, *peyos* behind his ears. When did he decide to grow *peyos*?"

Mirel smiled, which put Rabbi Landau at ease immediately. "Abba, Yehoshua has had *peyos* ever since he was a little boy!"

"Mirel, now I'm really confused. Didn't you tell me before you went out with Yehoshua that you absolutely would not consider a boy with *peyos*? And am I crazy, or was he without *peyos* when you married him?"

Mirel burst out laughing. "Abba, you're right about two out of three. You're right — I did not want a boy with *peyos*. And you're right — he did not have *peyos* when we dated and got married. But you are *not* crazy! Let me explain.

"Like I just said, Yehoshua has had *peyos* since he was three years old! All of his brothers have *peyos* — small ones behind the ear, just like him.

"The day he was supposed to meet you for the first time he needed a haircut. Now, normally, his roommate in the Yeshivah gave him haircuts. But that day his roommate wasn't there, so Yehoshua had to go to a barbershop. He asked for a regular haircut, and before he noticed what was happening, the barber had accidentally cut off one of his *peyos*! The barber apologized profusely, but it was too late. Well, you can imagine, Yehoshua was too embarrassed to meet you with only *one*, so he had the barber cut off the other one as well.

"Before the wedding, Yehoshua would have looked unkempt if he'd started to grow *peyos* again, so he decided to wait until afterwards.

"When Yehoshua told me that he was going to grow his *peyos* again, I had to laugh. It was something that mattered so much to me before we met, but mattered so little to me after we were married. Somehow I had always associated *peyos* with overly serious, somber personalities. Once I got to know how much fun Yehoshua is, I realized how silly I'd been.

"And when Yehoshua explained to me how he'd 'accidentally' lost his *peyos* on the day he met you, we both just marveled at the *hashgachah pratis* involved."

Rabbi Landau shook his head in disbelief. "*Mah rabbu ma'aseicha, Hashem!** Mirel, that's just amazing.

"This reminds me of what the Chazon Ish once said — that today there are no longer open miracles like there were in previous generations, with one exception: *shidduchim*. And the fact that Yehoshua 'accidentally' lost his *peyos* the day I met him is certainly an open miracle.

"And considering how discouraged you were feeling last year about *shidduchim*, I suppose it was also an open miracle that you agreed to go out with Yehoshua altogether," Rabbi Landau teased.

"Oh, Abba!"

*[as heard from Yaakov Feldheim,
Bayit Vegan, Yerushalayim]*

---

* "How great are your deeds, Hashem!" (*Tehillim* 104:24).

A Blessing
on Fruit

The late Gerrer Rebbe, Rabbi Simcha Bunim Alter, *zatzal*
(1888-1992), served as leader of the Gerrer Chasidim from
1977 until his passing on the seventh of Tammuz. The love
that he showed to all Jews was reflected in the enormous
crowd which turned out for his funeral, estimated at 175,000
to 200,000 people.

The Rebbe's sensitivity to the suffering of others was not
confined to human beings. For example, the water in his
apartment once became discolored and foul-smelling. The
plumber who was called eventually traced the problem to a
dead pigeon floating in the water tank on the roof of the
Rebbe's apartment building. In order to prevent a recurrence,
the plumber installed a stronger lid on the water tank.

Later that same day, the Rebbe was seen on the roof,
placing a bowl of water beside the water tank. When asked
about this he replied, "Just because I want clean water does
not mean that the birds have to suffer."

The Rebbe always tried to avoid receiving honor or material gifts of any kind. On the other hand, he always tried to
give to others as generously as he could. He gave freely of his
money, time, and blessings, but never at the expense of others.
For example, he insisted on paying for the total maintenance
cost for his apartment building as compensation for the
disturbance caused to his neighbors by the throngs of people
who came to see him.

In keeping with his love of all Jews and his boundless
generosity, he made it a practice of giving a piece of fruit to
everyone who came to see him. Some said this was done to

demonstrate *ahavas Yisrael* — love of his fellow Jew. Others said it was a sign of his humility, as if to say, "At least you should benefit in this way from your visit to me." Still others explained that when the petitioner made a blessing on the fruit at home, it combined with the blessing he received from the Rebbe to bring Heavenly blessings to fruition, so to speak.

The following story is an example of how a blessing made on the Rebbe's fruit brought about the realization of his blessing through remarkable *hashgachah pratis*.

✧   ✧   ✧

There is a Gerrer *kollel* student with a large family who lives in a tiny apartment on a narrow alley in the Zichron Moshe neighborhood of Yerushalayim. Let's call him Mordechai Weiss.

In spite of the financial hardships involved, Mordechai and his wife, Miriam, feel satisfied and fulfilled that Mordechai is still learning and pursuing his Torah studies in a *kollel*. With their large family of eight children, it is not practical for Miriam to work outside the home. However, the meager *kollel* stipend which Mordechai receives would never be sufficient to sustain their family.

What has made it possible for Mordechai to support his family is the additional disability pension which Mordechai receives from the Israeli government. Mordechai suffers from multiple sclerosis, which makes it impossible for him to work but does not interfere with his learning.

Mordechai has always seen his condition as a blessing and not a handicap. "If not for my condition," he would chuckle, "I would never be able to support my family."

Disability payments in Israel are issued through *Bituach Le'umi*, the national insurance program similar to American Social Security. Citizens pay into the system and also receive benefits from it, depending upon their income, health, and the size of their family.

Because Mordechai is unable to work, he is entitled to receive a monthly allotment which is based on the number of people in his family.

After his last child was born, Mordechai automatically received an increase in his monthly check from *Bituach Le'umi*. In spite of the increase, however, inflation was taking its toll on his fixed income. Mordechai and Miriam found themselves under considerable financial hardship; there simply was not enough money to make ends meet.

Miriam suggested that Mordechai appeal to his caseworker at *Bituach Le'umi* and ask for a hardship increase, something that is granted occasionally, but only in very rare cases. He knew that Miriam was right. He felt he had no choice.

The following day, Mordechai took his two canes and got on the bus. He arrived at the *Bituach Le'umi* office shortly before it opened and waited at the door. If he was one of the first ones in, he reasoned, he might not have to wait so long.

In spite of his plans, he still had to wait over an hour to see his caseworker. When Mordechai finally sat down inside the partitioned cubicle, he presented his case. "As you can see in my file, we now have eight children, *baruch Hashem*. And we simply cannot manage to feed them all on the allotment we are receiving. Therefore, we would like to request a hardship increase."

The caseworker nodded. "Yes, I can see what you mean, but the regulations do not permit me to authorize any increases without a home visit. Do you agree to that?"

"If that is necessary, then please come. When should we expect you?"

"I'm sorry, but I can't tell you that," the caseworker replied. "We are not permitted to inform the clients when the home visit will take place. You see, we can get a more accurate picture of the family's needs if no one knows when we are coming — although don't think for a minute that I doubt what you've said," he added.

Mordechai and Miriam were quite apprehensive about the upcoming home visit by Mordechai's caseworker. Their modest, overcrowded apartment would certainly substantiate their claim of inadequate funds, but the seriousness of the visit weighed heavily on their minds. If, for some reason, the caseworker should decide that they were ineligible for additional assistance, there would be no opportunity for appeal. The decision would be final.

Miriam suggested that Mordechai try to get in to see the Gerrer Rebbe and ask for a *berachah*. But Mordechai knew that the Rebbe was not well and therefore had curtailed his hours of receiving the public. Nevertheless, he agreed with Miriam that the urgency of the matter required every possible effort.

The next day, Mordechai made his way to the Gerrer Rebbe's apartment in Geula. While he waited in the small outer room with the crowd of other petitioners of all ages, Mordechai said *Tehillim* and prayed that he would be able to get in to see the Rebbe.

When his turn finally came, Mordechai stood up and grabbed his canes for support. With slow, laborious steps, he made his way into the Rebbe's study.

The Rebbe sat slumped in a large armchair, and he appeared to be drained and exhausted. Taking one look at the Rebbe, Mordechai realized that he would not be granted very much time.

As soon as the Rebbe looked up, Mordechai began speaking. He summarized his problem in a few terse sentences, spoken in a soft but pleading tone.

The Rebbe nodded his head slightly in response, as if he were reviewing Mordechai's situation. He closed his eyes briefly, like someone in pain. Then he reached for an orange and handed it to Mordechai. "Hashem will help," he said softly. "Go home and make a *berachah* on this, together with your family."

The Rebbe looked down and sighed, deeply. This signaled his attendant to escort Mordechai out. The *gabbai* turned to Mordechai and said apologetically, "The Rebbe is extremely fatigued today."

Standing once again in the Rebbe's waiting room, Mordechai looked down at the orange in his hand. *I had so little time with the Rebbe*, he thought. *I wish I had been able to explain my situation in greater detail. Perhaps if I had, the Rebbe would have given me more definite assurance. But, at least I have this fruit.*

Mordechai left the Rebbe's apartment. On the way home, he resolved in his mind to follow the Rebbe's instructions as literally as possible. Perhaps in the merit of his faith in the Rebbe's blessing, he hoped, his family would be granted the additional funds.

Later that afternoon, when all of his children had returned from school, Mordechai gathered his family around the table. He took out the orange given to him by the Rebbe, together with a plate and a knife. He ceremoniously placed the orange on the plate and then made the following announcement to his curious wife and children.

"Earlier today, my dear family," he began, "I received this orange from the Gerrer Rebbe, *shlita* . We shall now each have a chance to eat a little bit of this fruit. I shall cut up this orange into ten pieces so that we will all be able to make a *berachah* and taste some of it. Everyone please wait until I have finished cutting up the orange so we can all make the *berachah* together."

Miriam and all of the children watched quietly as Mordechai cut up the orange and handed the pieces out around the table. The novelty of the situation captured everyone's attention as each member of the family obediently followed Mordechai's instructions. Then the entire family recited the blessing and tasted the fruit.

A few days later, Mordechai received a letter from *Bituach Le'umi*. With trembling hands, he opened the letter and read it together with Miriam.

They both stared, with their mouths open, as they read the following letter:

Dear Mr. Weiss,

I came to make a home visit this week but did not come into your home. As I approached your apartment, I heard through the open window that you were sitting down to a meal with your family. I did not want to disturb you so I decided to come back later.

As I was about to leave, I overheard you telling them that you were dividing up a single fruit to share with your family.

Your financial distress was then quite evident to me. I no longer deem it necessary to come into your home to complete my assessment of your case.

Your request for additional assistance, therefore, has been approved. You shall be receiving the additional sum in your next check.

[as heard from Rabbi Dovid Finkelman,
Brooklyn, New York]

The Hat
Trick

Whether it is during the regular learning sessions or during the breaks in between, Rabbi Matisyahu Danziger* can always be found in the *beis midrash* of Yeshivah Ohavei Torah in Bnei Brak. (See "On the Bus.") He is either giving a *shmuess* (ethical lecture), counseling one of the *talmidim*, studying with a small group, or just learning by himself. So it is most unusual for Rabbi Danziger to leave the Yeshivah for any reason other than to go home.

But, as Rabbi Danziger often teaches his *talmidim*, there are times when a greater purpose can be served by closing one's Gemara in order to attend to someone else's needs. Such was the case one sunny Friday afternoon, not too long ago.

Rabbi Danziger's youngest son, Berel, had become a bar mitzvah one month before. He had delivered an extremely difficult and lengthy Torah speech, completely by heart. In addition, he had made a *siyum* on an entire tractate of *Gemara* at the bar mitzvah celebration. In order to reward Berel for these outstanding achievements, Rabbi Danziger offered to take him to the beach in Ashdod, which was half an hour's bus ride away from their home.

Of course, Berel could have gone to the beach with his friends. On Friday afternoons all Yeshivos are closed, and the long summer Friday afternoons allow plenty of time each week for boys to swim at the separate beach in Ashdod, which has

---

* All of the names in this story were changed by request.

men's hours every Friday.

Nevertheless, Rabbi Danziger understood that it would be a special treat for Berel to go to the beach with his father, and that it would be more important for him to reward his son with a trip to the beach than to remain in the *beis midrash* that particular Friday afternoon.

As Rabbi Danziger put it, "Giving a 13-year-old boy an afternoon alone with his father at the beach can sometimes accomplish more character refinement than giving him hours of ethical lectures."

Rabbi Danziger and Berel caught the 12:20 PM bus to Ashdod, a bus which often takes Orthodox men and boys each week to the separate beach. The new bus was full, although not overcrowded. But the chatter of the younger passengers made it seem as if it were bursting at the seams. Bottles of soda, bags of snacks and inflated beach balls and inner tubes seemed to protrude from everywhere as Berel and his father settled in for the twenty-five-minute ride to Ashdod.

Berel removed his hat and carefully placed it in the overhead rack above his seat. The hat still had the dustless look which proclaimed that its owner was a recent bar mitzvah boy. The gingerly manner in which he placed it on the rack also indicated that the novelty of wearing a hat had not yet worn off for Berel.

Rabbi Danziger looked on with satisfaction, as he noted the care with which Berel treated his new badge of maturity. It seemed a most opportune moment to teach Berel an important lesson.

"I'm very happy to see how well you take care of your hat," Rabbi Danziger began. "A *talmid chacham* must always give proper attention to his clothing because a neat appearance is a *kiddush Hashem* — a sanctification of God's Name."

The bus lurched forward and inched its way through the crowded city streets. Rabbi Danziger was still thinking about Berel's new hat when he suddenly remembered an incident which had taken place several years before, involving Aaron,

Berel's older brother.

"You were probably too young to remember when Aaron became bar mitzvah," he began.

"No, Abba, I do remember. We had the *seudah* in the shul across the street because the Yeshivah dining room was being painted."

"I see you do remember!" Rabbi Danziger was surprised. "Well something happened a few weeks later that you probably never even heard about — Aaron went into town to have his glasses fixed, and when he got on the bus, he took off his hat and put it in the rack above his seat — just like you did now. And since he wasn't used to wearing a hat, when he got off the bus he left without it!"

"Oh, no!" Berel exclaimed, enraptured by hearing this tidbit of family history. "What did Aaron do?"

Rabbi Danziger chuckled at the recollection, softened by the passage of time. "Well, first he tried to run after the bus to catch it. Then he called home and we contacted the bus company. In the end, we never found Aaron's hat."

"So what did you do?" Berel asked in suspense.

"I bought Aaron another hat!" Rabbi Danziger replied.

"Oh," Berel said, nodding, somewhat disappointed at the anticlimactic ending of the story.

"The reason I mention this now," his father went on, "is to point out to you how easy it is for a recent bar mitzvah boy to forget his new hat on a bus. So I hope you will make an extra effort to remember to take your hat when we get off!"

"Don't worry, Abba," Berel assured his father. "I'm not so absent-minded that I'd do such a thing."

Rabbi Danziger and Berel filled the short bus ride with cheerful conversation on a wide array of topics ranging from that week's Torah portion to Yeshivos for Berel to attend in the Fall.

After about twenty minutes, Rabbi Danziger decided to ask a fellow passenger how much longer it would be until they arrived at the Central Bus Station in Ashdod.

"Why do you want to get off at the Central Bus Station?" asked the man. "From what you're carrying, I can see that you're going to the beach with the rest of us."

"Yes, we are headed for the beach," Rabbi Danziger replied. "But don't we have to go to the Central Bus Station to get a local bus to the beach?"

"I suppose you could do it that way," the man acknowledged. "But it really isn't necessary to go all the way into town. Why don't you get off with me? There's a stop on this route which is in easy walking distance of the beach and will save you about 15 minutes."

"Thank you," said Rabbi Danziger. "I haven't been to the beach in quite a few years, and I didn't realize there was a quicker way. I'd appreciate it if you could let me know a little before we get to that stop so my son and I can get our things together."

"It's already too late for that!" the man replied, smiling and rising from his seat. "This is our stop."

Just then about half of the passengers grabbed their belongings and started to get off the bus.

"Quick, Berel, this is our stop!" Rabbi Danziger called.

Berel and his father jumped up and followed the other passengers who were bound for the beach.

As everyone crossed the road, the fresh smell of the sea indicated clearly that this was, in fact, the way to the beach. The group from Bnei Brak walked eagerly down the road, except for two bewildered people who stood at the curb looking at each other: Rabbi Danziger and Berel.

Yes..., Berel had forgotten his hat on the bus.

It took a few moments for Rabbi Danziger to figure out what to do next. Then he remembered that he had the phone number of Naftoli Roth, a former *talmid* who had become a lawyer and moved to Ashdod. There were no pay phones anywhere nearby so Rabbi Danziger decided to knock on the nearest door and ask if he could use the phone.

Naftoli was at home when Rabbi Danziger called and was delighted to hear his former Rebbe's voice. "Tell me where you're calling from and I'll be right over to pick you up." Naftoli took the address before Rabbi Danziger could even explain why he was calling.

A few minutes later, Naftoli was warmly greeting Rabbi Danziger and Berel. "If you came to Ashdod to go to the beach," Naftoli joked, "I'm afraid we're going to have a very short ride together."

Rabbi Danziger then explained to Naftoli that he and Berel had, in fact, planned to go to the beach, but since Berel had left his hat on the bus, their priorities shifted. Now they wanted to see what they could do to retrieve Berel's hat.

"No problem, Rebbe," Naftoli assured him, reaching into his back pocket for his cellular phone. "I can take care of that for you."

Naftoli took all of the details from Rabbi Danziger and then dialed the Central Bus Station. "Hello? Could you please connect me with the lost and found department?... Thank you... Hello, I'd like to report a lost hat... Yes, black... On the 12:20 from Bnei Brak to Ashdod... Yes, one of the new buses with those flat windshields... Thank you."

Naftoli placed the phone on his lap and turned to Rabbi Danziger. "They're looking for it now. Don't worry. I'm sure you'll get it back."

Naftoli picked up the phone again. "What? Of course I'm sure. It has to be there."

Naftoli suggested to Rabbi Danziger that they drive over to the lost and found office and have a look for themselves. Rabbi Danziger was reluctant to accept the favor, but Naftoli insisted, pointing out that the Central Bus Station was only a ten-minute drive from where they were.

At the Central Bus Station, the manager was not willing to allow anyone who was not an employee of the bus company into the lost and found room, but after a little verbal arm-twisting, Naftoli and Berel were allowed in. A thorough search was conducted, and the two emerged dejected and empty-handed.

Naftoli asked the manager where that particular bus would be parked, and he was told that since there would be no more buses traveling that route until Sunday, the bus was probably at the depot across town.

Naftoli got back into his car and quickly drove to the bus depot. When they arrived, they saw a huge lot filled with old buses. In the center of the lot was a large garage where buses were repaired. The entire lot was surrounded by a high fence. The place looked deserted, except for one religious worker who was locking up the main gate.

Naftoli rushed up to the worker and pleaded with him to allow them inside. He explained why they were there and pulled out some identification from his wallet. While the worker was looking at Naftoli's papers, Naftoli explained to Rabbi Danziger that due to the recent terrorist bombings of public buses, the security had been tightened at all depots where buses were parked overnight.

The worker was quite sympathetic, but he explained that it had been a mistake for them to come there since only buses that need repairs are brought to that particular depot. He then advised the threesome to return to the Central Bus Station and ask for Donni, who was the chief dispatcher and would be able to tell them exactly where the bus they were looking for was sent. Then he apologized for not being able to help, locked the gate, and walked to his car. Naftoli, Rabbi Danziger and Berel got back into the car without saying a word to each other. As soon as Naftoli pulled onto the main road, Rabbi Danziger broke the silence.

"I feel terrible that we have taken you on this wild goose chase after my son's hat. We've already wasted over a half an hour of your time. Surely you have more important things to do on an *Erev Shabbos* than run back and forth across town."

"Rebbe, please. I'm sorry you're in this predicament but there is nothing I would prefer doing right now other than help you find Berel's hat!"

"You are most generous with your time, Naftoli, but I simply cannot impose upon you any longer. Please do not bother taking us back to the Central Bus Station. It took close to twenty minutes to get here, and it will take another twenty minutes to get back. Just drop us at the beach and we'll worry about the hat after Shabbos."

"Rebbe, I haven't been a lawyer for very long, but so far in my practice I haven't lost a case. I'm not about to break my winning streak by losing Berel's hat. And anyway, I'm really curious about what this Donni fellow is going to be able to do for us."

Rabbi Danziger continued his protests as Naftoli continued to drive back across Ashdod toward the Central Bus Station. When they arrived, Naftoli jumped out of the car first and began asking around for Donni. By the time he found the right room, Rabbi Danziger and Berel had caught up with him.

"Excuse me, are you Donni?" Naftoli asked, almost in desperation.

A fortyish, balding man in an open-necked short-sleeved shirt looked up from the mound of paperwork covering his desk. He glanced at the threesome for a brief moment and then replied. "Yes, I'm Donni. If you're looking for the hat, Gershon Frank found it and took it home. You can pick it up now, if you like — here's his address."

Donni scrawled an address on a slip of paper and handed it to an open-mouthed Naftoli.

Back in the car again — but this time, all three were talking at once. How was the hat found? Was it really Berel's hat? How did Donni know they were looking for a hat? Who was Gershon Frank, anyway?

When they arrived at the address Donni had given them, all three jumped out at once. Naftoli knocked on the door. When the door opened, a familiar face greeted them. It was the bus company worker they had spoken to at the repair shop gate. He quickly went back inside and returned with Berel's hat.

Rabbi Danziger, Naftoli, and Berel just stared, open-mouthed, at the hat and then looked to Gershon for an explanation.

"I suppose you're all wondering how I found your hat," said Gershon, smiling broadly. "Well, after I left the repair shop, I began to drive home. While I was stopped at a red light in the center of town, I noticed one of the new square-front buses crossing the intersection right in front of me. And since I'm familiar with the routes to which all of our buses are assigned,

I knew that none of the new buses are assigned to local, intracity routes.

"So I said to myself, This must be an intercity bus that's being taken home for Shabbat by the driver. If so, perhaps it's the one from the Bnei Brak-Ashdod route on which you lost your hat.

"I jumped out of my car and stopped the bus. I flashed my photo ID to the driver and got on the bus. I didn't want him to suspect me of being a terrorist or a lunatic. Then I asked him if he drives the Ashdod-Bnei Brak route, and when he said, 'Yes,' I checked his bus and found your hat!"

Gershon chuckled. "You should have heard all the horns honking from all directions! Boy, were people angry with me for holding up traffic. But I was afraid if I let the bus go, I might not catch up with him later."

Rabbi Danziger, Naftoli and Berel all thanked Gershon profusely. Rabbi Danziger tried to offer Gershon a reward, but he adamantly refused to accept it.

Trying to distract Rabbi Danziger from insisting on a reward, Gershon continued his explanation. "So as soon as I got home, I called Donni. I knew I'd get home before you reached the Central Bus Station. I told Donni what happened and to expect three religious people coming to his office very soon looking for the hat which I had just found. I asked him to give you my address when you arrived."

Rabbi Danziger just couldn't stop thanking Gershon. And when they left Gershon's home, Rabbi Danziger couldn't stop thanking Naftoli.

And when he was finally relaxing at home that Friday night, he couldn't stop thanking Hashem for all the *hashgachah pratis* involved in retrieving Berel's hat.

"Just think — if Naftoli hadn't been at home, we would never have had a chance of finding your hat," Rabbi Danziger said to Berel, who was enjoying reliving the day's events with his father. "And if we hadn't been sent to the wrong depot by the manager, we would never have met Gershon — who found your hat! And because of the small detail that we were on one of those new buses, Gershon was able to recognize the bus we had taken to Ashdod!"

"And, Abba," added Berel, "just think of the *hashgachah pratis* involved in Gershon's car stopping at a red light *exactly* when the bus with my hat passed by!"

Rabbi Danziger and Berel just smiled at each other and shook their heads in awe.

[as heard from Rabbi Matisyahu Danziger, Bnei Brak]

A Bird
in the Hand

The blow torch ignited with a sudden pop, and the entire Elchonen* family gasped as much from surprise as from excitement. For the Elchonen children, the ignition of the blow torch signaled the start of a wondrous spectacle taking place in their own home. For Netanel and his wife, Elisheva, it meant that their kitchen was about to be made kosher.

Several hours later — after the stove, sink, and all the kitchen utensils had been kashered — Rabbi Baruch Fuchs took off his work gloves and sat down on a kitchen chair for a well-deserved rest.

"May I offer the Rabbi something to eat or drink?" Elisheva asked, her voice full of gratitude and appreciation.

"You certainly may!" Rabbi Fuchs responded. "I want the honor of being the first one to eat in your newly kashered kitchen. How about a cup of hot coffee?"

While Elisheva prepared the coffee, Netanel joined Rabbi Fuchs. "You must be exhausted," Netanel sympathized.

"Believe it or not, Netanel, I really enjoy doing this. For me, it's like a hobby. All week long I'm busy learning and teaching — purely intellectual pursuits. While they are certainly rewarding, there's nothing quite like the concrete gratification of physical work. When I put on these gloves and light up my blow torch, I know that I'm working towards a very tangible, and achievable, goal.

"My greatest satisfaction is to be able to look around at a newly kashered kitchen and know that all the food that will

---

* All the names in this story have been changed by request.

be prepared there now will be kosher. What can I tell you? For me, it's a real treat."

Elisheva brought three cups of coffee to the kitchen table. "I would love to serve you some cake with this," she apologized to Rabbi Fuchs. "But I haven't baked in the kashered oven yet!"

"All I want is a cup of coffee," he replied. "Working with that blow torch makes me pretty thirsty."

Rabbi Fuchs took a sip of his coffee and continued. "You know, one of the side benefits of doing this kind of volunteer work is that I get to hear some terrific stories. I'd enjoy hearing how you people decided to become religious. I know it isn't an easy step for a family to take."

"Rabbi," Netanel began, "if it hadn't happened to me, I wouldn't have believed it. But I don't want to keep you — you must be busy."

"Never too busy to hear things like this. And I asked *you*, remember? Hearing these stories strengthens my own *emunah* in *hashgachah pratis*."

"Okay, Rabbi," Netanel said. "I think you're going to enjoy our story..."

✧   ✧   ✧

Daniel Avir lives on the outskirts of Bnei Brak. His apartment building faces the crowded city, but behind the building is a huge, open field. Daniel likes the location of his home because it affords him the dual advantages of living in a large Orthodox community and still having wide-open spaces nearby.

One of the reasons Daniel prefers those wide-open spaces is that he and his pet are more comfortable that way. Daniel does not have a dog or a cat; he has a large, green, talkative parrot! Now, pets in general are not that common in Orthodox households, and certainly not parrots, but Daniel loves birds of all kinds. And living in a building on the edge of town means that fewer people can be disturbed by the occasional loud outbursts of squawking.

When Daniel first bought his parrot, he decided that he

would teach it to say only words or phrases that would be appreciated by his Orthodox neighbors. Eventually, with patient training, the parrot learned to say *Gut Shabbos* and *Shema Yisrael* and when asked, "How are you?" to respond with *Baruch Hashem*!

Once in a while, the parrot's squawking did disturb some of Daniel's neighbors, but the joy that the bird brought to the neighborhood children more than made up for the ruckus.

One day Daniel went up to the roof to check his solar water heater. The water was not coming out with the proper force and Daniel wanted to save the repair bill by fixing it himself.

Daniel stood on the roof with his parrot perched on his shoulder as usual. As the parrot squawked, "*Baruch Hashem! Gut Shabbos! Shema Yisrael!*" Daniel got to work on his do-it-yourself project.

As he was tinkering with the pipes, suddenly a gush of scalding water made him jump back. He was fast enough to avoid being burned but the parrot was badly frightened and flew away. It landed almost a mile away in an empty soccer field, dazed.

Netanel Elchonen was walking by the soccer field, when the bright green plumage caught his eye. When he walked over to investigate, he was amazed to discover the live, but greatly weakened, parrot. A gentle, nature-loving man, Netanel thought immediately of nursing the parrot back to health. His next thought was the delight he knew it would bring to his young children at home. Without hesitation, Netanel scooped up the limp parrot and took it home.

After a few days of tender loving care from the Elchonen family, the parrot began to regain its strength. By the end of the week, it was beginning to squawk with some of its former confidence, and after two weeks, it began to talk again.

On the morning that it shouted, "*Shema Yisrael Hashem Elokeinu Hashem Echad!*" Netanel couldn't believe his ears. He stopped short. Did this bird just say the *Shema*? he asked himself. A few minutes later Netanel's question was answered when the parrot repeated himself. There was no mistake! The bird had said the *Shema*.

After three days of this, Netanel was overwhelmed. "Elisheva," he said to his wife, "Do you realize that *I* don't even say the *Shema* — and here is an animal — a bird — reciting the *Shema* every day!"

Netanel just couldn't get over it. Although he was not at all religious and had never been religious, he knew enough to recognize the words of the *Shema*. And the thought of a bird saying these words, when he did not, bothered him more and more. Finally, he told Elisheva that he was thinking of attending morning services at the local synagogue, to say the *Shema* during the morning prayers. (He had attended services on rare occasions, so he knew that the *Shema* was recited daily.)

To Netanel's surprise, Elisheva was not only accepting; she was positively encouraging. "Of course you should go!" she said. "The parrot can say the *Shema* at home, but only a person can go to the synagogue!"

Netanel did go to the synagogue, and he felt so comfortable there that he decided to go back. Before long, he was a regular at the morning minyan. Eventually, Netanel began to feel embarrassed when he removed his yarmulka afterwards, outside. One day he left it on, and again, to his surprise, Elisheva expressed her approval.

Gradually, Netanel and Elisheva decided to have a Friday night Shabbos meal with the family, complete with candles and *Kiddush*. This led to a desire to keep Shabbos more fully, and eventually, to learn even more about Judaism.

Their thirst for knowledge led the Elchonens to an *Arachim* seminar for young Israeli couples. These seminars are designed to introduce interested non-religious families to Orthodox Judaism. For the Elchonens, the seminar only strengthened the commitment they had in fact already made.

The seminar included lectures by some of the *Arachim* instructors as well as workshops led by local volunteers. One of the volunteers was Daniel Avir.

During the refreshment break, Daniel mingled with the participants and socialized. As he introduced himself to each new person, if he learned that the person was from the area, he brought up the subject of his missing parrot. "Would you by any chance have seen a green parrot? I lost one a few months ago..."

When Netanel overheard Daniel asking people about the parrot, he realized immediately that this must be "his" new parrot. He didn't say anything to Daniel because he didn't want to return it, but nevertheless he asked around and got Daniel's name and address.

The next day, Netanel spoke to the Rabbi of his synagogue. "Do I have to return the parrot, Rabbi? We are all so fond of it, and my wife and I feel a special attachment to it because it is through this bird that we found our way back to Jewish tradition."

Netanel's Rabbi sat down and patiently explained that to return a lost object to its owner is a mitzvah from the Torah (*Devarim* 22:1-3). Since Netanel was learning and keeping more and more mitzvos, the Rabbi pointed out, this was a wonderful opportunity to fulfill a new mitzvah.

"And besides," added the Rabbi, "this bird was responsible for your entire family's return to Judaism; isn't it only right that you should practice what Judaism teaches by returning it to its rightful owner?"

Netanel agreed. The next day, he brought the parrot to Daniel, and explained what had happened.

Daniel was delighted to be reunited with his parrot, but he was even more pleased to learn how much his parrot had accomplished in its absence.

"I knew it was a good idea to teach my parrot the *Shema*," he told Netanel proudly, "but I never dreamed it was *such* a good idea!"

Rabbi Fuchs shook his head and sighed deeply. "I knew it was a good idea to ask what made you decide to become religious," he told Netanel and Elisheva. "But I never dreamed it was *such* a good idea!"

[as heard from Rabbi Benjamin Yudin,
Fairlawn, New Jersey]

Off the Wall

Some Yeshivos in Eretz Yisrael boast of spacious, modern buildings for classrooms and dormitories. Others, despite their intense dedication to Torah study, are somewhat less well endowed, and in fact, are so overcrowded that boys are forced to learn in the hallways for lack of space. One such Yeshivah is Yeshivas Minsk* in Yerushalayim.

Not every boy who applies to Yeshivas Minsk is accepted, but in spite of the large number of boys rejected, the Yeshivah is nevertheless bursting at the seams. As a result of this overflow enrollment, many of the *talmidim*, especially the ones from America, are forced to make their own arrangements for room and board. In order to keep the costs down, many of them rent old, small, relatively inexpensive apartments near the Yeshivah.

One of these "Minsker apartments," as they are called, is located in the Zichron Moshe neighborhood, within walking distance of the Yeshivah. Five boys were sharing a second floor, two-bedroom apartment during the summer of 1996: Aryeh Jacobi, from Boro Park; Sender Fischel, from Monsey; Yonasson Brander, from Baltimore; Avner Weinberg, from Flatbush; and Sruli Leiner from Kew Gardens, Queens.

Judging from the "architecture," it was clear that the apartment building was quite old. Neighbors explained that the apartment building was originally built without indoor plumbing, and that plumbing was added much later. In fact,

---

* All of the names in this story have been changed by request.

151

all of the houses on the narrow street were so dilapidated, that the boys were not surprised to learn one day during the summer that the building next to theirs was about to be demolished.

"I hope these Arab workers know what they're doing," said Aryeh, a tall, blond, soft-spoken twenty-one-year-old.

"You New Yorkers are always worried," chuckled Yonasson. "Do you really think this is the first time these guys have knocked down a building? I'll bet they do this every day."

Once inside their apartment, these two were soon joined by a third roommate, Sender, a round-faced young man with a broad smile and a neatly trimmed beard.

"You'd think they'd stop the banging during our afternoon break so we could get some rest!" quipped Sender to the other two.

"I wouldn't bet on it," replied Aryeh.

"Do you think it'll be like this every day?" asked Yonasson.

"I sure hope not!" Sender shot back. "Hey, anyone know how long it takes to demolish a building? I'm not going to do too well if I miss my afternoon nap every day. Wait till Avner and Sruli find out about this. They'll really be delighted."

"I don't think it will bother them as much as it bothers us," Aryeh observed. "The workers are banging right outside our wall. Avner and Sruli sleep in the next room so they're at least a little removed from the noise."

"Are you kidding?" asked Sender. "You can hear the pounding all the way up the block. Even before, when I was standing in the kitchen, it sounded as if they were banging on my head."

Aryeh, Sender, and Yonasson did not get much rest that afternoon and neither did Avner or Sruli. But the schedule of demolition did not include making loud noises every day between 2:00 and 3:30 PM, so the boys did manage to get a little rest during their afternoon breaks.

As the work of demolition proceeded, the roommates began to speculate on the quality of the work they were monitoring from the window of their apartment.

"If this job were being done in New York," Sruli commented

one evening, "it would have been completed in one day, two at the most. But these guys act as if they'll earn a bonus for every day longer they drag out the job."

"In New York they'd come with a bulldozer and finish the job in an hour," observed Sender, as he cleaned his glasses with one of his shirttails.

"I guess because all these buildings are attached to each other, they have to work slowly to prevent damaging the buildings on either side," added Yonasson.

"You mean," said Sender, "they have to be careful not to knock down *our* building by accident."

"Every time I hear the banging in our room," Aryeh confided, "I imagine the wall caving in on us."

Yonasson paced the floor nervously. "I don't think we really have to worry about that," he said, trying to reassure himself as much as the others. "Didn't you guys see the support beams they put up today? I'm sure those beams will secure the wall and prevent it from even cracking."

"That's what you *hope*," Sender shot back. "From the looks of those 'beams,' I wouldn't put much faith in them. They're barely thicker than broom handles. I just hope our *mezuzos* have been checked recently."

As the demolition continued, the five roommates paid close attention to the progress of the work. Aryeh even approached the foreman one day and asked about the safety of the wall his room shared with the building being demolished. The foreman reassured Aryeh that he had nothing to worry about. In fact, the entire job of demolition would be completed in only two more days, after which they would begin the rebuilding project that would strengthen that wall even more.

As promised by the foreman, the demolition was completed without incident. The same week, molds were prepared to hold the concrete for the new building. The five roommates in that Minsker apartment were as much relieved that they were now out of danger as they were relieved that the noise level of the work had dropped.

On Sunday afternoon, July 21 (the fifth of Av), at 2:45, the sleepy calm of that Minsker apartment was shattered by a grinding roar, as part of the wall adjoining the new building finally collapsed.

This was preceded only a few seconds by a series of cracking sounds which brought Avner, who was sitting in the kitchen at the time, to his feet. Instinctively, he rushed toward the affected room. Sruli, who had been sleeping in the next room, jumped up at the sound and followed right behind Avner.

Rocks, chunks of cement, and debris poured forth like water rushing through a broken dam. Thick dust filled the room, making it difficult to see inside.

Sender sat up on his bed, disoriented. He was completely covered with small rocks and crumbled cement. In panic and confusion, he kept yelling, "Ah! Ah! Ah!"

Sruli and Avner rushed in and saw the gaping hole where the wall had been, across the room from Sender's bed. They grabbed Sender and practically carried him into the kitchen. Sender, gasping for air, spoke incoherently. "What happened? Where am I? What's going on? What is this?"

As the dust began to settle, Avner, Sruli and then Sender peeked inside at the shambles. Heavy dust and crumbled rocks were everywhere. Both Aryeh's and Yonasson's beds, which lined the damaged wall, were covered with pieces of broken stone and chunks of cement and plaster. Both beds were buried under the weight of the rubble. Only Sender's bed was still standing under the relatively lighter weight of fragments that had flown off the wall and across the room.

As the three young men stood there counting their blessings that they were not hurt, the construction foreman rushed in to see if everyone was all right. He apologized profusely for the accident and then added his praises to Hashem for the good fortune that no one was hurt.

After the foreman left, the three roommates began the arduous task of going through the clothing and personal items in the room to assess the damage. They had not yet even thought of how to clean up the mess when Sender blurted out,

"Hey, where are Aryeh and Yonasson?"

Together with Avner and Sruli, Sender began to wonder out loud why their other two roommates were not in the apartment when the wall caved in.

"Usually they're sleeping at this time," Sender noted, out loud. "If Aryeh and Yonasson had been in their beds like they usually are, then when the wall gave way they would have..." Sender's voice trailed off. He couldn't even express the horrifying thought.

"They're usually the first ones to lie down during break," added Sruli. "It's not like either of them not to come back to the apartment."

"Whatever kept them away today, really saved them. I can't wait to hear where they were," said Avner.

Where were Aryeh Jacobi and Yonasson Brander on that hot afternoon during the Nine Days, the period of mourning preceding Tishah b'Av, during which misfortunes are almost expected? What had kept them off their ill-fated beds during that one afternoon break? What *hashgachah pratis* had spared them?

Yonasson Brander had little exposure to the world of secular Jewry. He was born and raised in the very Orthodox, Yeshivah community of Baltimore, Maryland. He had always attended Yeshivos and socialized only with the boys in his school.

After spending almost two years at Yeshivas Minsk, Yonasson had begun to think about his insulated lifestyle. He was aware of the work of numerous outreach organizations which brought the message of Torah Judaism to unaffiliated, non-religious Jews, and he admired the work of the "*kiruv* professionals" who spent their days and nights trying to win back these lost souls.

But Yonasson was in a dilemma. He believed very strongly that the most important endeavor he could pursue was the study of Torah, that anything else was secondary. But at the same time, he yearned to participate in the *kiruv* movement, to be able to take part in the important work of bringing secular Jews back to a Torah way of life.

Yonasson kept his dilemma to himself. He feared that his friends might tease him about his longing to participate in outreach activities. In addition, he knew of no way to get involved in *kiruv* without compromising his commitment to full-time learning.

At the end of June that year, Yonasson had noticed a wall poster that grabbed his attention. It was as if the words flew out and hit him in the face:

> *Seeking: full-time Yeshivah students to work as counselors at Orthodox summer camp for non-religious American and Israeli boys 8-13 years old.*

It was the last line that really convinced him to act:

> *Camp program is for bein ha-zemanim (Yeshivah summer vacation) only.*

Yonasson quickly wrote down the telephone number and stuffed it into his pocket. Later, he questioned himself. Even though he would not have to miss any time from his learning, was he really cut out to be a camp counselor for non-religious boys? Would he be a help or a hindrance? Perhaps he should just relax during his vacation like his friends were planning to do?

Yonasson wrestled with these thoughts for a couple of days, and then decided to make the call. He asked a few questions and liked what he heard. This seemed to be the opportunity he had been waiting for — now he could get involved in *kiruv* without missing any learning.

He arranged to go for an interview, which would take place at the camp office in Ezras Torah and was scheduled for 2:30 PM...on the afternoon of July 21.

Aryeh Jacobi also had a dilemma. He had been learning for a almost a year in Yeshivas Minsk and he loved it. He had great *chavrusos* and the *shiurim* were wonderful, and given by outstanding Rabbis. He had made many new friends and had become closer to his Israeli cousins. But most of all he simply loved just living in Eretz Yisrael.

If it were up to Aryeh, he would have chosen to learn in Yeshivas Minsk forever. But his parents had other ideas. They wanted him to come back to Boro Park to begin dating. It was time to get married, they told him. Aryeh wanted to listen to his parents, as he always did — but he also wanted to stay in Israel. Aryeh decided to present his dilemma to a well-known Rabbi who was also a friend of the family.

The Rav told Aryeh that in fact he did not have to choose between the two options — he could have both. "Go home, temporarily, until you become engaged," he said. "Then you can return to Eretz Yisrael and learn here at least until the wedding — and hopefully afterwards as well."

Aryeh took the Rav's advice and returned home for Pesach. As if the Rav's words had been prophetic, he became engaged within a month and then returned to study in Yeshivas Minsk until his wedding, which was scheduled for right after Sukkos.

During the summer, Aryeh began to anticipate his upcoming wedding in greater detail. "I suppose," he told himself, "sometime during the Shabbos before the wedding or the week of *sheva brachos* I'll be asked to say a *d'var Torah*. I might as well take advantage of my free time now to prepare something to say that will bring honor to my parents and pride to my in-laws."

Aryeh did not want to work on his *d'var Torah* during his regular study sessions because that might inconvenience his study partners, who depended on him. Therefore he decided to remain in the *beis midrash* and to devote time to this independent study only during his afternoon break, between 2:00 and 3:30 in the afternoon...and the day Aryeh actually started was Sunday..., July 21.

[as heard from Aryeh Jacobi, Boro Park, Brooklyn]

Doorway to Life

Let's stop here at the two dots," Rabbi Leff said, looking up from his *Gemara*. "Then, *b'ezras Hashem*, we can try to finish the *perek* at tomorrow's *shiur*."

Rabbi Leff reluctantly closed his *Gemara* and took a well-deserved sip from the cup of coffee on the table in front of him. He sighed with satisfaction at being able to give this daily class to the working men at Moshav Matityahu, where Rabbi Leff still serves today as Rav, *Mora d'Asra*, and *Rosh Yeshivah*. But he was even more pleased with the dedication of his students, who managed to squeeze in this one-hour *shiur* between *Shacharis* and their busy work day.

"Excuse me, Rabbi," said Chagi shyly as he approached Rabbi Leff, together with a few members of the class. "May we speak with you for a moment?"

"Why certainly, Chagi. What is it?"

"Well, Rabbi, we wanted you to know that it is going to be difficult for some of us to continue coming to the *shiur*, at least for the next few weeks."

"I'm sorry to hear that. What's the problem?"

"As you know, many of us who attend the *shiur* work in the vineyards in the morning," Chagi began.

Rabbi Leff nodded.

"Well, next Monday," Chagi went on, "we'll be starting the pruning. That means we'll have to be out in the vineyards by 7:00 AM, which will be impossible if we attend the *shiur* after *daven*ing."

"Look, Chagi, of course I understand. Since this is a

moshav shitufi (a collective agricultural settlement), you must each take your turns at doing the necessary work. I'll definitely miss you all at the *shiur*, but I realize that this is unavoidable."

"Uh, that's actually what we wanted to discuss with you, Rabbi. We really don't want to miss your *shiur* — even for a few weeks. So we'd like to ask you if it would be possible to switch the *shiur* to *before davening*, rather than afterwards. That way, we'd be able to continue learning with you. We've already spoken with everyone else who attends and they said it would be all right with them. So now we want to ask if you would also agree..."

"But, Chagi, that means we'd have to start the *shiur* at 5:30 in the morning! Are you sure you wouldn't mind getting up that early?"

"Rabbi, if you can manage it, we can too. We really don't want to give up Torah learning at the start of the day."

Rabbi Leff looked around at the expectant faces of his farmer-students. "It would be an honor and a privilege for me to deliver the *shiur* before *davening*," he replied. "In fact, I'm so impressed with your commitment to learning, that I don't feel worthy of being your Rav!"

The men surrounding Rabbi Leff all broke out in embarrassed smiles at the compliment they had just received.

Rabbi Leff then finalized the agreement. "So it's now official. Starting on Monday, the *shiur* will be at 5:30. Chagi, please be sure to post a sign on the bulletin board so any potential newcomers will be informed of the schedule change."

Monday morning, the 6th day of Shevat, 5747 (1987), Rabbi Leff woke up early. He glanced at the clock on his night table and saw that it was only 5:00 AM. Too early to get up, he thought to himself as he rolled over on the other side.

For a brief moment, he thought he smelled something burning. But he quickly reassured himself that it was probably just the benign smell his electric heater often gave off on cold winter mornings.

As Rabbi Leff tried to go back to sleep, he reminded himself of the new schedule for the *shiur*, which was starting that morning. I really don't need half an hour to get ready for shul, he thought to himself, as he deliberated about getting out of bed. But then again, this is the first morning we're starting at 5:30. Maybe I should get started early, just to be sure I'm not late.

In the past, 5:00 AM would have been a full hour before Rabbi Leff had to be in shul. But this day, because of the new schedule, it was only half an hour before he had to be there — so he decided to get out of bed.

As Rabbi Leff walked out of his bedroom toward the bathroom, he passed the room where four-year-old Matis-yahu, three-year-old Menachem, and one-year-old Sarah Orah were sleeping.

He stopped and stared at the black smoke oozing out around the doorway.

Rabbi Leff flung open the door and rushed into the smoke-filled room. Huge flames leapt up the walls on all sides. Frantically, he tried to douse the flames with the water in his *nagel vasser* bowl, which he still held in his hands, but the fire was already too advanced to be stopped so easily.

"Rivka! Rivka!" he yelled, waking his wife, and together they grabbed the still-sleeping children out of their beds, to safety. Along the way, they called out and woke the older children, fourteen-year-old Miriam and thirteen-year-old Devorie.

Although he was awakened by the shouts, eleven-year-old Shimi thought he was dreaming and having a nightmare, but he was quickly convinced that the danger was quite real and that he had to leave the house *at once.*

In what seemed like hours, but was barely a minute, the entire Leff family had gathered on the lawn in front of their burning home. Rabbi Leff took a quick head count and saw that everyone was there. Then he went back into the flaming building to see what he could salvage before it was too late.

Neighbors were already rushing with the fire extinguishers as Rabbi Leff ran into the inferno. Billowing black smoke clogged the hallways of the Leff home. The heat was so intense that Rabbi Leff was forced back outside almost immediately. Then he and his family stood by helplessly and watched as the trained village volunteers gradually brought the blaze under control.

Not only has Rabbi Leff not forgotten those miraculous events, but he welcomes the opportunity to retell them. "Don't we say in our prayers three times a day, '*L'dor va-dor nodeh lecha u'nesaper tehillasecha*' (From generation to generation, we thank You [Hashem] and tell over Your praises)?"

After consulting with the *posek ha-dor* (leading halachic authority of our generation) Ha-Rav Yosef Shalom Elyashiv, *shlita,* Rabbi Leff made the sixth day of Shevat an annual family *yom tov.* On that day, all family members who were in the house at the time of the fire, fast. In the evening, they all put on their Shabbos clothing and sit down to a festive meal, to which the poor are invited. Special *Tehillim* are recited at this personal *seudas mitzvah,* following the guidelines set by Rav Avraham Danzig, *zatzal.**

"If my *Gemara shiur* had not been rescheduled for 5:30 that morning," Rabbi Leff points out today, "I surely would have gone back to sleep when I woke up at 5:00 that morning. Of course, the smoke and flames might have awakened me a little later anyway, but had I lost even a couple of minutes my wife and I might not have had enough time to get all of the children out safely, *chas v'shalom.* So the fact that the *shiur* was rescheduled starting *that very morning,* was nothing short of miraculous.

"But that was not the only *hashgachah pratis* involved here," Rabbi Leff adds. "The door to my youngest children's bedroom frequently got stuck on the carpet. Sometimes it was so tightly locked in place that only the smallest children could get in and out. We usually managed to force it open all the way periodically so my wife could get in to clean up! But then a few weeks later it would get stuck again. It was such a hassle trying

---

* See *Chayei Adam, Hilchos Megillah,* chap. 155, para. 41.

to open it further that we often just left it as it was and let the little children squeeze in at night and out in the morning.

"For three whole weeks before the fire, that door was in its "stuck position." We had worked so hard opening it all the way up the last time, that we were not in a hurry to go through that bother again.

"My late father-in-law, *alav ha-shalom*, came to visit with us that Sunday, *the day before* the fire. When he was living in the States, before he retired and made *aliyah,* he had owned a carpet business, so he was very familiar with such problems and also quite handy with tools. When he came to our home that day he decided to fix the door which was always stuck.

"Now bear in mind, my father-in-law had been to our home on many previous occasions when that door was jammed. He had seen how difficult it was to open and never said anything about it. You know how it is with things around the house that are broken or in need of repair — people just get used to them and learn to accept things the way they are.

"But for some reason, which obviously was *hashgachah pratis* at work, my father-in-law decided that day that he was going to repair the door. He simply took out some tools, rolled up his sleeves, and had the door swinging freely in less than an hour.

"Sometimes I think about what might have happened if my father-in-law had not fixed that door when he did. Then I imagine a terrifying scenario: me struggling desperately with the door, as black smoke pours out of the burning room. Such thoughts bring tears of joy and gratitude to my eyes, and I rejoice all over again for the great kindness Hashem bestowed upon me and my family."

[as heard from Rabbi Zev Leff,
Moshav Matityahu]

The Proper Englishman

Some adjectives just seem to modify certain words, automatically, such as: "cold" and "beer," "hot" and "tea," "black" and "umbrella."

For me, the words "proper" and "Englishman" make another pair of words that are practically married to each other.

The phrase "proper Englishman" took on a special meaning for me the first time I visited London in 1968. I was on my way back to New York after spending a year learning in Eretz Yisrael. (See "A Chassidic Tale" in *AiSHeL*, for more details of that year.)

My friend, with whom I was traveling, and I heard that our travel agent could arrange for a stopover in London for a few days at no extra charge. We jumped at this golden opportunity to do some sightseeing.

On the *motza'ei Shabbos* we were in London, we took a bus to the Underground (what the subway is called in England) and went downtown to look around. Both of us lost track of the time. So, when we finally decided to head back to our hotel room, we caught one of the last trains going in our direction. It was only after we boarded the train that we learned that public transportation in London stops at around midnight on *motza'ei Shabbos* — like Yerushalayim but unlike New York City! Luckily, we also managed to catch the last bus back from the train station to our hotel.

We had to go about seven or eight stops on the bus. By the third stop, the red double-decker bus was completely full, with all the seats occupied and three or four people standing in the narrow aisle on the lower level of the bus.

At the fourth stop, only one person got off, but there were at least half a dozen people waiting to board the bus. As they started to approach the bus, the conductor who collects the fares gently told the wide-eyed would-be bus riders, "Sorry, all full up."

One brave, assertive Englishman protested lightly, with a tremor in his voice, "All full up?"

"That's right," replied the conductor matter-of-factly. "Only allowed to 'ave two in the aisle and I've got three standin' there already."

With that, he reached up and gave a tug on the line that ran along the ceiling of the bus and rang a bell in the driver's cab, signaling him to drive on. Then six very disappointed, long-faced but *proper* Englishmen politely remained at the curb as this last bus pulled out into the street.

Had this scenario unfolded in any other country, it would have taken much more than, "Sorry, all full up," to keep the almost stranded travelers off that bus. In many other countries, the irate would-be riders might have stormed onto the bus and even thrown off the conductor, if necessary. But in London, this curbside queue of proper Englishmen barely winced or expressed any discontent whatsoever. They merely remained on the sidewalk and politely watched the last bus of the night drive off down the road...without them.

✧   ✧   ✧

Manny Davis* is a proper Englishman. In his large, knitted *kippah* and open-necked white short-sleeved shirt, however, he looks more like an Israeli than an Englishman. In fact, he is both. He now lives in the thriving town of Efrat, having emigrated from England twelve years ago.

Although his dress and lifestyle have changed dramatically since his earlier days in London's Golders Green neighborhood, Manny still retains his British accent and deportment.

---

* All the names in this story have been changed by request.

"Have you got a spot of tea?" Manny politely asked his wife, Penina, not too long ago.

"Sure thing," Penina chirped from the kitchen.

When the two were seated together at the dining-room table, Manny discussed his plans to purchase a minivan for the family. As they now had seven children, it was no longer possible for the family to travel anywhere together, unless they went by bus. Their old sedan was simply too small to transport the entire Davis family. They needed a larger vehicle and a minivan seemed like the perfect solution.

Once the minivan was purchased, Manny insisted that his children treat the upholstered interior as they would their living-room furniture. "No sticky fingers on the seats," he warned them, "and certainly NEVER any shoes!"

Raising one's voice was always prohibited in any Davis car. And it goes without saying that wearing seat belts at all times was at the top of the list of proper conduct in transit.

Manny and Penina ran such a tight ship that they did not need to repeat the minivan rules too often. Their children were accustomed to following rules at home. They were also used to wearing their seat belts and speaking softly in the old jalopy. So the new minivan rules of cleanliness did not faze any of the Davis children.

One Friday, shortly after the minivan was purchased, Manny and Penina took three of their children with them on a short trip to the local shopping center.

Even with the strict rules of conduct, the Davis children always loved to go along for the ride whenever they could. It was fun to go anywhere in the new minivan.

Manny and Penina stocked up on fruits, vegetables, and various purchases for Shabbos and then headed home. The back row of seats in the minivan was filled with their children, while the middle row of seats was loaded with groceries.

As the minivan pulled onto the street where the Davises live, Manny called back with authority, "All right, children, unbuckle your seat belts and come up front to get some of the bags. Everyone is to carry something into the house. Don't expect me and Mum to carry all of this inside by ourselves."

The minivan was still moving as the three Davis children obediently followed their father's instructions. Now it was highly unusual for Manny to allow his children to unbuckle their seat belts before the car came to a complete stop. And it was even more uncharacteristic of Manny to ask them to get up and move forward while the vehicle was still moving.

What made Manny break his own rules? Why was he suddenly flexible about his "seat belts at all times" policy? How come this proper Englishman was encouraging his children to behave improperly?

The answer to these questions came in a flash.

No sooner had the children gotten up and come forward than they heard the loud crack of a gunshot followed by the crunching sound of breaking glass. Manny reflexively slammed on the brakes and whirled around. He found himself staring open-mouthed at two bullet holes in the rear side windows. In between was a neat tear in the upholstery of the back row of seats, running from one side of the van to the other.

It was immediately clear to Manny what had happened. A bullet had entered one window, whizzed across the back of the seat, and gone out through the opposite window. He shuddered in fright at the realization that followed.

The path of the bullet was *exactly* where his three children had been sitting only seconds before! Had he waited to tell them to get up until the minivan stopped, *as he always did,* his children would have been sitting just where the bullet ripped through the upholstery.

A short while later, after the minivan was parked and the Davises had returned home and calmed down, Manny made some inquiries and learned that the shot had been fired by an Israeli policeman who was chasing a suspected criminal. It was highly unusual, and even against Police Department protocol, for a policeman to fire his revolver under such circumstances, and especially in such a residential area where innocent bystanders could be hurt.

Even though the Davis children were not protected by police regulations, they were clearly guarded by the One Who watches over us, constantly.

Hashem is gracious and righteous; and our God is compassionate. Hashem watches over the simple [the children*].

TEHILLIM 116:5,6

[as heard from Rabbi Nossi Spitzer, Kiryat Unsdorf, Yerushalayim]

---

* The *Gemara* explains that "simple" in this verse refers to children. See *Sanhedrin* 110b, as well as *Yevamos* 12b, 100b; and *Kesubbos* 39a.

In the Bag

In the 1950's, it was not uncommon to see the heartbreaking sight of young children wearing heavy braces and walking with crutches. These unfortunate victims of the polio virus were born before the discovery of the Salk vaccine. Today, *baruch Hashem*, as a result of that discovery, polio has been relegated to a mere footnote of medical history.

Learning disabilities are certainly not as crippling as polio was, but they are even more pervasive. And as with any scientific or medical breakthrough, those who were born after the discovery of the diagnosis and treatment of a disorder benefit in ways that could not even have been imagined before.

Today, for example, there are learning centers and clinics where learning disabilities can be properly diagnosed, as well as a great variety of special education programs and schools where children with such disabilities can be properly taught and then often mainstreamed into regular classes and schools. The former nightmares of ridicule, failure, and shame are being eradicated today for many children who have learning disabilities.

✧ ✧ ✧

Unfortunately, this was not the case when Amnon* started school in the 1960's. At that time, few teachers and hardly any parents had ever even heard of the term "learning disabilities." There were good students and poor students. And often the poor students were trouble-makers. So when Amnon's parents

---

* Not his real name.

were told by his second-grade teacher that he did not seem to be paying enough attention, they automatically assumed that their son was lazy.

Amnon's father worked long hours for the Postal Authority and was not able to attend the parent-teacher conferences at school. But he valued his oldest child's education enough to make sure that his wife, a part-time clerical worker, did meet with Amnon's teachers.

As Amnon went through the public school system in Cholon, the reports from the teachers were always the same: Amnon could be doing better work. He does not pay attention. He never completes his homework. He is disruptive in class.

Amnon's parents took these reports quite seriously. At first they tried to bribe him to improve by promising him special trips. When that failed, they used threats of punishment. And when that too failed, they often resorted to berating him and shouting at him, more out of their own frustration than out of a genuine conviction that it would lead to any improvement in Amnon's academic performance.

By the time Amnon was a teenager, it was clear that he was not going to finish high school. His parents reluctantly agreed to let him take a part-time job as a stock boy at a local warehouse.

Instead of teaching him responsibility, however, the job brought him into contact with friends of whom his parents strongly disapproved. The job also provided Amnon with more pocket money than his parents would have wanted him to have at his age. Amnon used all of the money he earned to buy cigarettes and beer and to go to the movies with his new friends.

As Amnon entered his mid-teens, his parents had less and less influence on his behavior. They wanted Amnon to attend youth-group meetings and activities, to socialize with more goal-oriented youth. But Amnon preferred the company of those teenagers who hung out on street corners and in coffee shops.

It was about this time that some of Amnon's friends introduced him to drugs. At first it was just some mild drugs at a party given by a friend of a friend. A few months later, he experimented with more serious drugs at another party. And by the end of the year, he was a full-fledged addict.

Because of his substance abuse, Amnon was rejected by the army and could not do the normally compulsory military training. So while other eighteen-year-olds were beginning their three-year stint in the Israeli army, Amnon was sinking further into his decadent life of drugs and, eventually, petty crime.

In order to support his drug habit, he found it necessary to steal. His lifestyle precluded holding down a regular job, so his only access to money was criminal.

Amnon's relationship with his parents was extremely strained. Finally, following a particularly heated confrontation with his father, Amnon moved out of his parents' home and moved in with one of his friends.

Learning from his friends and from experience, Amnon became somewhat adept at picking people's pockets — especially tourists. His typical *modus operandi* was to team up with two partners who would stage a loud argument with each other in the street outside a hotel. The two accomplices would exchange insults until one would throw the other to the ground. As a crowd gathered, the one on the ground would scream and cry until an even larger crowd was there. After a few minutes, he would simply get up and walk away. By then, Amnon usually had succeeded in picking more than one pocket of the curious onlookers who had gathered.

Even pickpockets and drug addicts need some time off for rest and relaxation. So Amnon liked to go to the beach whenever he wasn't "working." There he could stretch out and doze, blending in and getting lost among the nameless masses on the sand.

But just as many businessmen can't help reading stock reports while on vacation, Amnon could not pass up a golden opportunity whenever he encountered one.

It was a warm afternoon in the early summer of 1997, that

Amnon found himself sitting at the crowded beach in Tel Aviv and staring at a brightly colored, unattended beach bag.

For sure it belongs to a tourist, Amnon thought to himself as he scanned the beach in all directions looking for the owner. I'll bet it contains lots of expensive items from abroad, he mused.

Amnon began to contemplate stealing the bag. But he was enjoying himself at the beach. If he were to steal the bag, he'd have to leave immediately. On the other hand, if he didn't take the bag right now, the owner might return and his window of opportunity would be shut tight.

Amnon also considered his current financial situation. He had only a few shekels left in his pocket and would need to buy more drugs by tomorrow. That tipped the scale. He would go for the bag.

In one fluid motion, Amnon picked himself up off the sand and scooped up the bag at the same time. As if the bag had always belonged to him, Amnon jauntily swung it freely, as he briskly walked away from the water towards the closest exit.

Once he was on the street, Amnon stole his first glance over his shoulder to see if he was being pursued. To his relief, he was not being followed or even noticed.

It was then that Amnon relaxed enough to note how heavy the bag was. Doesn't feel like the weight of a bag one would bring to the beach, he thought to himself, as he dodged around the corner, distancing himself from the scene of the crime.

Slightly out of breath and with mounting curiosity as to what his newly acquired bag contained, Amnon stopped, leaned against a lamppost, opened the bag, and began to inspect the contents. It was then that he first noticed the tangle of wires at the mouth of the bag.

Clearly this was no tourist's bag. The weight of the bag, combined with the strange-looking wires, led Amnon to conclude that someone more experienced than he should be examining the contents. Now he was more concerned for his safety than for the few shekels he might make.

Looking up, Amnon noticed a security guard standing just inside the main entrance of a luxury hotel. Now, there's someone who might be more familiar with these things, Amnon thought to himself.

"I just found this on the beach," Amnon explained to the guard. "Perhaps you should have a look at it."

The guard hesitatingly accepted the bag from Amnon and looked inside. Immediately, he called for his supervisor with his walkie-talkie. The supervisor then called the bomb squad of the Police Department.

The lobby of the hotel was soon sealed off. No one was allowed on the sidewalk in front of the hotel and all vehicular traffic was stopped in both directions. Local residents were unperturbed, as finding a *chefetz chashud* (suspicious object) was not an uncommon event in Tel Aviv, in the wake of recent terrorist attacks. Usually the objects turned out to be harmless.

This time, however, the experts quickly determined that the contents of Amnon's bag were, in fact, a terrorist bomb, timed to go off in another seventeen minutes. The bomb was quickly defused and then the officials at the scene allowed the media in to get their story.

"Who found the bomb, Captain?" a television reporter on the scene asked.

"That man in the blue shorts with the small pony tail," replied the bomb squad supervisor, pointing to Amnon.

An impromptu news conference was suddenly arranged in a corner of the hotel where Amnon had turned in the beach bag. "How does it feel to know that you saved dozens of innocent lives today?" the reporter asked Amnon, as the camera crew jockeyed for the best position from which to record Amnon's statement for the evening news.

Amnon groped for the right words. "Well, I just did what had to be done," he explained, feeling awkward about his instant stardom.

Amnon was a hero. The next morning his picture was splashed across the front page of every daily newspaper in Israel.

"Amnon was not at all the type of person you would expect to be responsible for saving dozens of lives and preventing possibly hundreds of injuries," Rabbi Hanoch Teller observes, a few months after this episode.

"It certainly illustrates incredible *hashgachah pratis* that Amnon should be on the beach that day and steal the bag containing the bomb. But this incident also epitomizes the well-known *mishnah*: *"Ein lecha adam she'ein lo sha'ah —* There is no man who does not have his hour" [*Pirkei Avos* 4:3].

"On this *mishnah*, the Rambam writes, 'It is not possible that every man does not have some time when he can harm someone or benefit him, even in a small way.'

"And in this case," Rabbi Teller continues, "Amnon benefited the citizens of Tel Aviv in a very great way."

Rabbi Teller hoists one of his small children onto his lap as he adds, "I can't think of a better illustration of this *mishnah*. This episode really reminds me of how much we should respect the unlimited potential of every Jew to help others... And this story also reminds me of how much we must also be grateful for the ever-present protection of *Ha-Kadosh baruch Hu* (The Holy One, blessed is He)."

[as heard from Rabbi Hanoch Teller,
Arzei ha-Birah, Yerushalayim]

Meeting with a Master

The best way to perfect a skill is to observe the work of an expert. This is true for any craft or any art. Interested in improving my story-telling ability, I arranged a meeting with a master story teller, Rabbi Noach Weinberg, *shlita,* the *Rosh Yeshivah* of Aish Hatorah in Yerushalayim.

Our meeting was scheduled during the summer of 1996 and took place in Rabbi Weinberg's spacious and well-appointed study. The large, impressive room faces the Western Wall plaza in the Old City of Yerushalayim and the view from his picture window is magnificent, awe-inspiring, and absolutely breathtaking.

Rabbi Weinberg greeted me warmly with an outstretched hand and a friendly smile. I explained that it was he who had motivated me to write this book and that I was looking for more stories of *hashgachah pratis* in Eretz Yisrael. He was delighted with the whole idea and immediately began the story telling for which he is so well-known.

In order to capture the full flavor of the three stories Rabbi Weinberg shared with me that afternoon, I will present them in the first person, as I heard them from him.

✧   ✧   ✧

Speaking of *hashgachah pratis,* do you know that Hashem also has a sense of humor? I recall a boy who came in to one of our beginners' programs who had just come from visiting the Kosel for the first time. This young man was not only non-re-

174

ligious; he was also quite anti-religious. He came from a completely secular, American Jewish home and he was, as he said, "turned off" by all of the religion he was exposed to here in Yerushalayim.

He had come to the Kosel thinking of it more as a tourist attraction than anything else. You know — how can you go back home and say that you did *not* visit the Western Wall?

So he walks into the area where people are *davening* and the attendant insists that he put on one of those paper yarmulkas. He has no choice and grudgingly puts it on.

Then he approaches the Kosel to get a look up close. All around him men are *davening.* Some are saying *Tehillim;* many are praying out loud; some are swaying back and forth. And he just can't take it! This is just too much for him — too much religion, everwhere he goes. He's had it!

He grabs the yarmulka off his head and throws it down to the ground in disgust. And then...as soon as he bares his head, one of those holy doves that fly around the Kosel drops down some business that hits our boy right on the top of his head! He looks up to Heaven and thinks to himself, Okay, so You got me back.

At that very moment, Rabbi Meir Schuster comes over and asks him if he'd like to visit a Yeshivah. Ha, ha, ha! He was afraid to say, "No!"

The miracles of *hashgachah pratis* are with us each and every day, in Eretz Yisrael as well as in the Diaspora. Of course, there's no doubt that you can *feel* the *hashgachah* more here than anywhere else, but unless someone is ready to believe in Hashem, even miracles won't affect him.

Let me give you an example. We had a young man who came into one of our programs for Israelis about ten years ago. Let's call him Uri. I don't really remember why Uri came. I think he was part of a group that came in all together and he'd decided to tag along.

The seminar leader was discussing the subject of miracles and asked the group if they had ever experienced any. Some members of the group shared a few stories and then Uri said he would like to tell us what had happened to him.

Uri was an outdoor enthusiast who loved to go hiking with his friends. One day he's on a hike in the desert, in the Negev, somewhere outside of Beersheva.

Apparently Uri didn't take care to drink enough during the couse of the day and after a few hours he began to feel faint and ill. One of his companions, a medic, recognized the symptoms of dehydration and began to worry. He knew that Uri was in danger and he regretted not bringing along the first-aid kit which he always took when he accompanied organized groups. It contained a special saline solution infusion for such circumstances.

As Uri began to feel worse and worse, his friends decided to fan out in a desperate effort to find help. As they frantically ran in all directions, one of Uri's friends spotted something shiny lying on the ground. He stopped out of curiosity and bent down to see what it was.

There, in the dust, lay an unopened saline infusion kit! Apparently an organized group of hikers, accompanied by a medic, had passed here and lost it.

The friend rushed back, handed the kit to the medic who administered the first aid, and saved Uri's life.

The entire seminar was silent. You could have heard a pin drop. Uri turned to the seminar leader and confessed, "I believe that the chances of finding a saline solution kit in the middle of the desert are less than one in a million. I also believe that without that infusion I would not be here today. It was surely a miracle. But, nevertheless, I still cannot believe in God."

So even if your life is saved by an unbelievably miraculous event, if you want to stubbornly hold on to your disbelief, even miracles cannot stop you.

Of course, most people are not as stubborn as Uri was. For most people, experiencing a miracle *can* change their lives. Sometimes the miracle is life-saving in a physical sense, and sometimes in a spiritual sense. In this last story, the *hashgachah* of my meeting someone here at Aish Hatorah combined with a miracle in America to bring someone home to his roots.

1 remember that I was sitting right here at this desk and minding my own business when someone knocked at my door. My secretary must have been away from his desk so I answered the door myself.

A young man with a knapsack on his back entered the room. Let's call him Reuven. He asked me, "Are you the *Rosh Yeshivah* here?"

I told him that's what some people call me, and I invited him inside. Once we were sitting, he turned to me and asked bluntly, "What's the purpose of a Yeshivah?"

I thought to myself, Where is this guy coming from? I couldn't figure out what he wanted with this question. But I thought that if *hashgachah* brought him to my door, there was a reason. So I answered, "You tell me — what do you think the purpose of a Yeshivah is?"

Reuven puffed up his chest and proudly explained, "The purpose of a Yeshivah is to provide an opportunity for man to get closer to God. Isn't that right, Rabbi?"

"Well, yes, you could say so," I told him.

"So if that's the purpose of a Yeshivah," he went on smugly, "I just want you to know that *I* don't need a Yeshivah. You see, God does miracles for me. Me and God are like *this.*" Reuven held up his hand with his middle finger wrapped around his forefinger to indicate how close he felt to God.

I told Reuven that I was very moved to be in the company of someone who was so close to God. There was a brief silence. Then I gently asked him how exactly he knew that he was so close to God.

"Oh, Rabbi, that's easy to explain," Reuven eagerly began. "Like I said, God does miracles for me. Let me give you an example. My favorite hobby is riding my mountain bike all over the countryside back in the States. So one day I'm riding my bike down a quiet, narrow mountain road, and all of a sudden, out of nowhere, a speeding car comes up the hill, barreling around a curve and heading straight at me.

"To my left is the solid rock of the mountain. To my right is a steep cliff with a low guard rail. And coming head on is the speeding car.

"I have no choice but to veer off the road to my right. I try to stop but I'm going too fast.

"My bike flies right over the guard rail like a ski jump. I sail over the cliff and drop straight down about fifty feet. I'm in such a panic I just yell, 'God!' on my way down.

"My bike lands between two huge rocks and gets twisted like a pretzel. And I walk away with barely a scratch anywhere on my body.

"Now, I ask you, Rabbi, wouldn't you call that a miracle? Doesn't that prove to you that me and God are like this?" Again, he held up his hand to show me his middle finger wrapped around his forefinger.

I told him that I could not argue with him — that was a miracle if I'd ever heard one. To save him like that God must surely love him, I added.

Reuven was feeling pretty good about himself and had this self-satisfied look on his face. He got up to leave and I waited until he was just about at the door when I called him back.

"Reuven," I said, "I fully accept that it was God who saved your life that day in the country. But I would like to ask you something else."

"Sure," Reuven said, confidently. "What would you like to know?"

"Who do you think it was who threw you off that cliff in the first place?"

Reuven just stood there with his mouth open.

Then I suggested to him that perhaps the very same God

who saved him from the fall had brought the speeding car from around the bend. I went on to ask him why he thought that God would do such a thing — why put his life in danger only to save him?

Reuven just shook his head.

Then I answered my own question. I told him that perhaps God was trying *to get his attention.* That maybe this was a wake-up call. I waited a moment and then asked him if he wanted God to try again to get his attention...

Reuven stayed to learn in our Yeshivah.

When I left Rabbi Weinberg's study I headed for the Kosel to say some *Tehillim* and *daven Minchah.* I wanted to keep alive the glowing inspiration I had just received from Rabbi Weinberg's stories of *hashgachah pratis.*

On the way down the long, winding stone staircase, I reflected on the *hashgachah pratis* of my having attended Rabbi Weinberg's public lecture on *kiruv* fifteen years earlier, which eventually led to my writing this book (see Preface). I also pondered the *hashgachah pratis* of my being able to get a private appointment with Rabbi Weinberg that day. All of this made me appreciate even more so how every step we take...every day and everywhere...is constantly guided by the benevolent gaze of *einei Hashem.*

Glossary

The following glossary provides a partial explanation of some of the Hebrew and Yiddish (Y.) words and phrases used in this book. The spellings and explanations reflect the way the specific word is used herein. Often, there are alternate spellings and meanings for the words.

ASHKENAZIM: Jews of Eastern European descent.

B'EZRAS HASHEM: "with God's help."

BA'ALAS CHESED: a woman of kind deeds.

BARUCH HASHEM: "Thank God!"

BASHERT: (Y.) destined; meant to be.

BAYIS NE'EMAN B'YISRAEL: an everlasting Jewish home.

BEIN HA-ZEMANIM: the semester break in a Yeshivah.

BEIS MIDRASH: the study hall of a Yeshivah.

BITACHON: trust in God.

CHESED: loving-kindness.

D'VAR (DIVREI) TORAH: brief sermon(s) on a Torah subject.

DAN L'CHAF ZECHUS: to judge others favorably.

DAVEN: (Y.) to pray.

EMUNAH: faith in God.

FREILICHE: (Y.) happy; joyful.

HACHNASAS ORCHIM: hospitality.

HA-KADOSH BARUCH HU: The Holy One, blessed is He.

KALLAH: a bride.

KEVER: a grave.

KIPPAH: a skullcap.

KIRUV: bringing closer to Jewish tradition and observance those who are far from it.

KOLLEL: an academy of Torah study for grown, mostly married, men.

LASHON HA-RA: malicious gossip; slander.

MA'ARIV: the evening prayer service.

MECHANECH: an educator; a teacher.

MECHILAH: forgiveness.

MENAHEL: a director; a principal.

MIDDOS TOVOS: good character traits.

MINCHAH: the afternoon prayer service.

MOTZA'EI SHABBOS: Saturday night.

NIGGUN: a tune; a Chassidic melody.

PEYOS: sidelocks.

PUSHKE: (Y.) a collection box.

REFUAH SHELEMAH: "[May you have] a complete recovery."

SANDAK: the person who has the honor of holding the baby during the bris.

SEPHARADIM: Jews of Spanish or Oriental descent.

SEUDAH: a festive meal.

SHACHARIS: the morning prayer service.

SHECHINAH: the Divine Presence.

SHEVA BERACHOS: the seven blessings recited at a wedding; one of the festive meals held in honor of the bride and groom during the week following the wedding, at which the seven blessings are recited.

SHIDDUCH: a marital match.

SHIUR: a Torah lesson; a class.

SHLITA: a Hebrew acronym for the words, "May he live a long and good life, Amen."

SHTREIMEL (-LACH): (Y.) traditional fur-trimmed Chassidic hat(s).

SIDDUR (IM): prayer book(s).

SIYUM: the celebration held upon completing the study of a Talmudic tractate.

SUKKAH: the temporary booth that is dwelt in during the Festival of Sukkos.

TALMID CHACHAM: a Torah scholar.

TALMID (IM): student(s).

TEFILLAH (-LOS): prayer(s).

TZEDAKAH: charity; righteousness.

YESHIVAH BOCHER: (Y.) a Yeshivah student.

YISHUV: a Jewish settlement in Israel.

ZATZAL: a Hebrew acronym for the words, "May the memory of a righteous one be for a blessing."

ZECHUS: privilege; merit.